Farmed Out

Farmed Out

Agricultural Lobbying in a Polarized Congress

CLARE R. BROCK

Oxford University Press is a department of the University of Oxford. It furthers
the University's objective of excellence in research, scholarship, and education
by publishing worldwide. Oxford is a registered trade mark of Oxford University
Press in the UK and certain other countries.

Published in the United States of America by Oxford University Press
198 Madison Avenue, New York, NY 10016, United States of America.

© Clare R. Brock 2024

All rights reserved. No part of this publication may be reproduced, stored in
a retrieval system, or transmitted, in any form or by any means, without the
prior permission in writing of Oxford University Press, or as expressly permitted
by law, by license, or under terms agreed with the appropriate reproduction
rights organization. Inquiries concerning reproduction outside the scope of the
above should be sent to the Rights Department, Oxford University Press, at the
address above.

You must not circulate this work in any other form
and you must impose this same condition on any acquirer.

Library of Congress Control Number: 2023042424

ISBN 978–0–19–768380–4 (pbk.)
ISBN 978–0–19–768379–8 (hbk.)

DOI: 10.1093/oso/9780197683798.001.0001

Paperback printed by Marquis Book Printing, Canada
Hardback printed by Bridgeport National Bindery, Inc., United States of America

CONTENTS

Acknowledgments vii

1. Too Many Cooks in the Kitchen: Bitter Partisanship and Uneasy Alliances 1

2. A Growing Policy Area: The Creation of Agriculture as a Staple of American Politics 19

3. Work Hard for the Money: Polarization and Evolving Lobbying Strategies 31

4. The (Not Quite) Business as Usual of Washington: Corporate Lobbying Strategies 55

5. Keeping Up with the Corporations: Interest Group Adaptation to Party Polarization in Congress 76

6. He Said, She Said: The Power of Interest Group Negotiations 94

7. Money, Money, Money: The Link between Influence and Wealth 109

8. Influencing a Polarized Congress: Herculean or Sisyphean? 124

CONTENTS

Appendix A: Notes on the Quantitative Methods 143

Appendix B: Notes on Qualitative Methods 151

Notes 155
References 161
Index 181

ACKNOWLEDGMENTS

This book grew out of my dissertation; as such, the people to whom I owe appreciation are numerous. First and foremost, I want to acknowledge my children—Everett and Oliver—without whom I might have written this book much more quickly but also much less joyfully, and my husband, Justin Toungate, without whom I could never have done this at all. It is to the three of them that I dedicate this book.

I owe an enormous debt of gratitude to my colleagues and friends, Vivienne Born, Wouter van Erve, Courtney Buchkoski, Jamie Parker, and especially Parker Hevron, who named this book. I also want to thank my Chair, Jonathan Olsen, and the rest of the Department of Social Sciences and Historical Studies at Texas Womans University for their support and encouragement. I greatly appreciated the kindness and feedback that were offered to me during my time in the department. I have been allowed to create Food Politics, Money and Politics, and Public Policy courses that overlapped with my research, and my students in these courses have been generous enough to listen as I talked about the issues I care about— probably far too much.

I also want to extend thanks to Christopher Bosso for the incredibly detailed notes on my manuscript, as well as Sam Workman, Darrell Lovell, Dana El Kurd, Wouter van Erve, and Stuart Soroka, all of whom read chapters during the process of writing this book, and to the anonymous reviewers who took the time to carefully read and consider my work. Good scholarship is not generated in a vacuum, and the feedback

I received from friends, colleagues, and reviewers has made the work here more rigorous and better written than anything I could ever have produced on my own. Thanks also to my former dissertation committee—Batt Sparrow, Bryan Jones, Sean Theriault, Brian Roberts, and John Mark Hansen—who oversaw the initial work out of which this book has grown.

This book could not have been written without the cooperation and generosity of those who I interviewed. Most are anonymized, but regardless, every lobbyist, journalist, and staffer who I spoke with was incredibly generous with their time and knowledge.

Angela Chnapko, my editor at Oxford University Press, deserves particular recognition as well. She has been enthusiastic about the project as well as patient in response to my many questions and frequent worries.

Finally, over the many years during which I have been working on this project, my parents, Marilyn and Stephen Brock, and my sisters Hannah, Petra, and Nora, have all offered me invaluable support—from listening to my venting and providing babysitting services, to encouragement and cheerleading. I also want to thank the friends who have promised to buy the book, and particularly, Rachel Navarre and Jessica West, who allow me to text them constantly for emotional support and funny memes.

There are many others who have helped me, encouraged me, supported me, and read my work along the way, some of whom I have likely forgotten to mention here by name. Please know that you all have my gratitude and undying thanks, even if I didn't write it here specifically.

Too Many Cooks in the Kitchen

Bitter Partisanship and Uneasy Alliances

How did pizza become a vegetable? We should start with the premise that food in America is affordable, abundant, and of generally high quality. Sometimes. But visit your neighborhood school cafeteria and you might begin to question that statement. School lunches are often brown, mushy, too salty, too sweet, and over-microwaved. Breakfasts are often pre-packaged, fortified sugar in "pastry" form. And comically, it is better now than it once was. Most adults can remember, with some horror, the school lunches from the 1980s and the 1990s; sides that came in plastic wrap, limp pizza, and slimy "salads." These lunches are also the only reliable meals that some school children will eat, meaning that their appearance, flavor, and any attached stigma may act as further barriers to creating genuinely hunger-free schools.

The US Department of Agriculture (USDA) sets the national standards for school lunches. These standards are intended to provide well-balanced meals that include fruits, vegetables, and essential nutrients, especially for those children who may face food insecurity at home, away from the fluorescent lights of the school cafeteria. And while parents and students alike complain that the food offered is subpar, schools must provide food on a large scale within a tight budget. Operating with just a dollar and change per child, per day, schools have to purchase, prepare, and provide lunches to students with a wide variety of nutritional and dietary needs

Farmed Out. Clare R. Brock, Oxford University Press. © Clare R. Brock 2024.
DOI: 10.1093/oso/9780197683798.003.0001

(Siegel 2019). To supplement the stingy budget of the National School Lunch Program (NSLP), the USDA also offers free provision of certain commodity crops to schools. Rather than being oriented toward current health recommendations, the USDA website says that "these purchases help to stabilize prices in agricultural commodity markets by balancing supply and demand" ("Food Distribution" n.d.). Schools cannot afford to turn down the commodities offered for free by the USDA to supplement school lunches, regardless of what the offering might be; so, public schools find themselves in a sticky predicament with a limited budget, free (but not of their choosing) commodity foods, and often unhappy parents and students. How did we get here?

As detailed previously, the earliest school lunch programs emerged during the early 1900s haphazardly across the country; in some areas, mothers, teachers, or civics groups provided free meals to poor children, while other schools used the lunchroom as an opportunity to teach their home economics classes domestic skills (Levine 2008). The first real, coordinated federal efforts to create a uniform school lunch program began during World War II, as the federal government began providing school lunches across the country intended to reduce malnutrition and increase the number of healthy young men able to serve in the military. As the war drew to a close, a school lunch coalition formed to lobby for the preservation of the school lunch program, arguing that the federal government "has a stake in the future of all the children" (Levine 2008, 52). For several years, the responsibility for providing school lunches bounced between federal agencies, but in June 1946, Congress created the National School Lunch Program (NSLP). The program was a triumph, not only for anti-hunger activists but also for the nation's farmers. The new lunch program would feed hungry children while supporting struggling farmers with the federal purchase of commodity crops. The program grew, over the decades, housed in the US Department of Agriculture, and continued to represent an uneasy alliance between child welfare advocates and agricultural interests.

Fast-forwarding to 2008 and the election of President Barack Obama, child nutrition became a centerpiece of the administration. First Lady

Michelle Obama visited *Sesame Street* in 2009 and taught Elmo about healthy habits—eating a healthy lunch, taking a walk, reading a book (*Sesame Street* 2009). The episode was hopeful, wholesome, and generally adorable. She also created the White House Kitchen Garden on the South Lawn to "initiate a national conversation around the health and wellbeing of our nation" and launched the Let's Move! campaign to encourage kids and families to "lead healthier lives" ("Let's Move: Achievements" n.d.). In 2010, as part of the Obama administration's initiative to reduce childhood obesity and improve national health, the Healthy, Hunger-Free Kids Act was passed with strong bipartisan support and signed into law. The law focused on strengthening nutrition standards for school meals and offering incentives for the creation of farm-to-cafeteria programs. The legislation was initially a hit—who can argue with lunch ladies? And the "lunch ladies," represented by the School Nutrition Association, were definitely for it. But even in the earliest phases of rulemaking and implementation, cracks began to form in the bipartisan support for the new health standards. A little-known feature of the modern school lunch program is that relatively few cafeterias have working kitchens, and those that do are often woefully out-of-date or feature subpar equipment (Upton and McAuliffe 2019). Much of the food served in cafeterias across the country is created elsewhere and then shipped, pre-packaged, to schools and simply microwaved before being placed on trays and handed out. In other words, frozen food manufacturers have a lot of skin in the game when it comes to school lunch standards.

As the Healthy, Hunger-Free Kids law was fleshed out into actual regulations, interest groups began to mount opposition to new standards and restrictions. The American Frozen Food Institute aligned with the potato lobby and, together, objected to many of the new standards that were aimed at reducing school reliance on "starchy vegetables" (Confessore 2014). Senator Susan Collins (R-ME) became a particularly vocal critic of the starchy vegetable restrictions, as Maine is one of the top potato-producing states. Meanwhile, a full-fledged battle began raging over how a proposed rule for tomato sauce would count toward the developing vegetable requirements. The USDA initially ruled that two tablespoons of tomato paste would count as two tablespoons of tomato paste, a seemingly obvious and innocuous rule (what else would tomato paste count as?). However, the Schwan Food Company (a company that incidentally manufactured around 70% of all pizza sold in American schools) privately and strongly objected to this categorization. Schwan argued that tomato sauce should be considered a vegetable, as it is made from tomatoes. The company also objected to requirements that would reduce sodium in school lunches, which it argued would make the food bland and tasteless (Confessore 2014).

The potato and tomato lobbies were powerful, and successful. When the law took effect in July of 2012, French fries (formerly potatoes) and pizza (saucy!) were notoriously counted as vegetables in the lunch line. While the new rules regulating school lunches may have improved nutritional standards, students across the country took to social media to complain about their meals (Confessore 2014). Very quickly the School Nutrition Association (SNA), aligned with a variety of conservative groups and lawmakers, began lobbying for a rollback of the nutrition standards established by the law (Overby 2014). This startling about-face from the SNA, supposedly frustrated with food waste and complaints from schools, made the group one of the most vocal and credible critics of the Healthy, Hunger-Free Kids Act. *Politico* reported that the SNA receives about half of its $10 million operating budget from food industry members, though the group firmly denies that such partnerships motivated its sudden opposition to legislation it previously supported (Evich 2014).

In 2013, the USDA began on a new round of rulemaking aimed at snacks, and the conflict between the proverbial lunch ladies and the White House intensified. New regulations were set to target "competitive" foods, like those sold in vending machines, or food sold by outside vendors such as Chick-fil-A or a variety of pizza franchises. By May of 2014, the conflict had escalated, and Robert Aderholt, a Republican from Alabama, attempted to use the annual appropriations process to legislate a waiver that would allow schools to avoid many of the strictest regulations. When the legislation came to the House appropriations committee, with a waiver provision intact, almost all Democrats voted nay, making it "the most partisan vote in the history of the National School Lunch Program" (Confessore 2014).

The Obama administration threatened to veto any legislation containing a waiver, and opposition to the waiver solidified from other sources as well. While the SNA supported the waiver, claiming that cafeterias were operating at a net loss and needed "a temporary reprieve to allow schools to catch up" (Aubrey 2014), it is of note that nineteen former presidents of the SNA opposed the waiver and aligned themselves with Michelle Obama in asking Congress to reject it (Overby 2014); and more than two hundred organizations, including the American Medical Association, environmental groups, and food advocacy organizations, signed a letter opposing a waiver (Confessore 2014). The American Heart Association's CEO, Nancy Brown, is on record saying that "by giving special interests a seat at the school lunch table, some members of Congress are putting politics before the health of our children," though this is perhaps an ironic statement coming from someone who herself represents a special interest (Aubrey 2014). Margo Wootan of the Center for Science in the Public Interest (another interest group opposing the waiver) issued a statement saying, "The House waiver proposal is an attack on kids' health dressed up as a favor to schools. . . . Perhaps it's more a favor to the pizza companies, French fry makers, steel can manufacturers, and any number of corporate special interests that think the school lunch program is their own ATM" (Aubrey 2014). In a victory for the administration, the Senate Appropriation Committee's bill did not include waiver legislation, and ultimately health advocates were (at least, temporarily) able to block any significant changes to the Healthy, Hunger-Free Kids legislation (Schwartz and Wootan 2019).

Since implementation, the new standards set by the Healthy, Hunger-Free Kids Act have largely remained, though there have been some minor rollbacks, particularly under the Trump administration. But understanding how such popular, bipartisan legislation moved from golden-child status to a source of bitter partisan tension is primarily a matter of understanding interest groups and their legislative allies. It also makes the important point that "interest groups" are not a monolith; there are often many, many interest groups involved in advocacy on any given piece of legislation, and the extent to which they have influence will depend on a great many factors—the public mood, ideological conflict and conflict expansions (who gets involved?), salience and attention to the issue, and more. And at the end of the day, Congress (not lobbyists) decides.

THE SECRET FARM BILL THAT WASN'T

In the summer of 2011, while interest groups, agencies, and members of Congress were debating over the details of implementing new school lunch standards, congressional leaders began playing a game of chicken over raising the federal debt limit; specifically, the newly elected conservative House majority intended to use the looming deadline to raise the debt limit as a tool to force spending cuts in the federal budget. In August, just hours away from a federal shutdown, congressional leaders in the House and Senate agreed to extend the debt limit through January 2013 in effort to reach a compromise and avoid default. Their plan involved the creation of a House-Senate "supercommittee," which would recommend a new budget and cut the deficit by at least $1.2 trillion over ten years (Bosso 2017, 77). The new supercommittee was given the power not only to make cuts to the budget but also to change specific existing programs.

The supercommittee was immediately seen as a venue for authorizing, essentially, a "secret" farm bill without being forced to go through a public and protracted negotiation process of reauthorization, since the 2008 farm bill was set to expire in 2012. By late fall of 2011, the leaders of the House and Senate agriculture committees were "working feverishly" to draw up a proposal for a new farm bill to be subsumed into the supercommittee proposal and to potentially create five more years of food policy "without so much as a spirited debate" (Bittman 2011). And in October, Debbie Stabenow (D-MI), Frank Lucas (R-OK), Pat Roberts (R-KA), and Collin Peterson (D-MN) recommended an agriculture package to the supercommittee that would include billions in cuts from across the farm bill, including cuts to commodity programs, conservation programs, and nutrition programs, together with new work requirements (Bosso 2017, 78). In an opinion piece for the *New York Times*, Mark Bittman (2011) described the dilemma this entire bizarre new order of operations posed for policy advocates: "This leaves many advocates and progressives in the world of food, environment, health and poverty in the odd position of trying to influence the group of four's report to the supercommittee while hoping the process fails." Advocates, it turned out, got what they were hoping for. The supercommittee collapsed, unable to reach any kind of deal, and with that the leadership's hope of avoiding a public farm bill debate died quietly. With the expiration of the 2008 farm bill looming, the agriculture committees began their normal process of holding hearings and considering how to reform the farm bill in the spring of 2012.

Interestingly, in the failed supercommittee process, commodities were the main focus for potential cuts, rather than nutrition—but by late 2012 and into 2013, the Nutrition title would become the lightning rod for major cuts to the farm bill. The attempt to negotiate a "secret" farm bill highlights a tactic that has become increasingly common in Congress and represents a strategy that has proved very attractive to leadership—restrict information and debate, and rush legislation through committee or floor consideration as quickly as possible (Curry 2015, 3).

This story—like the story of the Healthy, Hunger-Free Kids Act—illustrates the messy, complicated, highly conflictual and protracted challenges of lawmaking in a highly partisan environment—in which the extremes are pulling away from the middle and pushing a difficult agenda; but it adds the caveat that interest groups, no matter how much information, brainpower, and pressure they apply, are not (at the end of the day) in the room where it happens, so to speak. Interest groups who are on the receiving end of policy—benefits or burdens—are ultimately still at the whims of Congress. This means a continued presence and lobbying efforts for as long as it takes the legislature to move. And in today's world, sometimes that is a *long* time; in fact, the farm bill reauthorization discussions that began in 2011 did not result in legislation until early 2014, nearly two years after the 2008 farm bill was set to expire.

FOOD FIGHTS: CREATING A MESS OF AGRICULTURAL POLICY

Similar stories of conflict, hyperpartisanship, and interest group jockeying can be told of nearly every piece of agricultural or food policy considered since the mid- to early 2000s. The only way to make sense of this messy, contradictory, paradoxical food system is to understand the policymaking process and its relationship to interest groups. Decades of literature, like *Gaining Access* by John Mark Hansen in 1998, to *The Rise of the Agricultural Welfare State* by Adam Sheingate in 2003, to *Framing the Farm Bill* by Christopher Bosso in 2017, has studied how interest groups shape the agricultural policymaking process in the United States. With each of these bodies of work it is increasingly clear that lobbying is a powerful force on our food system. In fact, it is not too bold a claim to say that the food system is a product of lobbying: anti-hunger lobbying; environmental and climate lobbying; animal welfare lobbying; worker rights and safety lobbying; corporate profit lobbying; big farm subsidy lobbying; lobbying for and against sugar protections; lobbying for and against milk protections; immigration reform lobbying; slaughterhouse regulation lobbying; bee and pollinator protection lobbying; and so much more. Every five years (give or take) the farm bill is up for reauthorization, and the contents of that legislation are shaped nearly as much by lobbyists as by legislators. But, beyond the world of food and agriculture, the political landscape has been shifting rapidly. Everything from healthcare, to voting rights, to financial industry reform has been subject to intense partisan warfare, and food has not been spared from the encroachment of partisan battles.

In fact, because food is so deeply cultural, it often becomes a signifier of identity and is used in political battles that are only indirectly related to food or agriculture. In a discussion about Alexandria Ocasio-Cortez's (D-NY) proposed "Green New Deal," Fox News's Jeanine Pirro claimed, "Do you like red meat? . . . Not so fast. The left with their Green New Deal wants to make sure you don't" (McCarthy 2021). Lauren Boebert (R-CO), meanwhile, claimed that the Green New Deal was going to restrict Americans to just four pounds of meat a year, and tweeted, "Why doesn't Joe stay out of my kitchen?" (Boebert 2021). The proposed Green New Deal was never going restrict Americans to eating just four pounds of red meat a year, but that wasn't really the point. Rather, food is part of our cultural heritage and identity, and therefore it is also a useful talking point as partisanship increasingly becomes a meta-identity, encompassing and overlapping with nearly all other aspects of our identities (Mason 2018). The connection between partisanship, identity, and food is only becoming more tightly linked as partisanship becomes a more powerful meta-identity; the way our food is regulated, produced, consumed, and marketed are all, therefore, fair game for partisan warfare.

Food and agriculture policy are primarily made in farm bills, but it is not *only* made in farm bills. Nonetheless, the food fights that center around farm bills are essential to understanding how food policy evolves in the United States. Chapter 3 returns to the story of the secret, not secret 2012, 2013, ultimately 2014 farm bill whose reauthorization was being debated while conflict raged over the Healthy, Hunger-Free Kids Act regulations. In 2013, what eventually became the Agricultural Act of 2014 failed in the House for the second time in two years. The failure shone a spotlight on the tension between Republican House leaders, who were pressing for cuts to food stamps and toughened work requirements for recipients in a bid to please the Freedom Caucus and other far-right members of the party, and Agriculture Committee Chairman Frank Lucas (R-OK), who warned that such measures would kill Democratic support for the legislation (Rogers 2013). With House Republican leadership on one side, the Agriculture Committee on the other, and Democrats on a different playing field altogether, interest groups swarmed. The conservative Heritage Foundation actively tried to kill the farm bill outright, while another conservative organization, the Secretary's Innovation Group, suggested an amendment that would give states more freedom to restrict the Supplemental Nutrition Assistance program (SNAP) through additional work requirements (Rogers 2013). Food banks and anti-poverty groups simultaneously lobbied to stop work requirements and SNAP cuts, and budget watchdog groups teamed up with a seafood trade group to repeal a catfish inspection program at the Agriculture Department (Nixon 2013).

Meanwhile, health advocates and anti-hunger advocates found themselves in conflict over whether or not SNAP reauthorization should include restrictions on the types of foods that could be purchased with the cards; for instance, many nutrition advocates wanted to restrict SNAP funds from being used for soda purchases, while anti-hunger advocates worried that any curtailing or restrictions would be used against the program as an excuse to further cut funding (Fisher 2017). And these conflicts were not pleasant or pretty; anti-hunger advocate Jessica Bartholow articulated the fight, saying, "The public health community is using poor people as pawns to get at soda companies. What they're doing is just as vicious and evil as what Paul Ryan wants to do to poor people" (Fisher 2017, 107).

The furor of lobbying, the repeated failure of farm bill legislation in 2013, and the conflict between committee leadership and House leadership all raise important questions about what is happening to the proverbial iron triangle, in which much of policymaking is dominated not by political parties or president but by cozy (and sometimes not-so-cozy) relationships among like-minded legislators, bureaucrats, and interest group leaders. The recent fight over school lunches certainly did not look cozy, and yet a relatively small number of voices often seemed to command an outsized influence over the debates, while the conflict between committee and party leadership reflected the new reality of hyperpartisanship and polarized politics. How are lobbyists and legislators working together in this brave new world of partisan acrimony? This book addresses the question of how agricultural and food policy is created and passed under such conditions, who has outsized influence, and why.

POLARIZATION, LOBBYING, AND POLICY CREATION

Interest groups have a tremendous impact on public policy in two important ways. First, they effectively act as adjunct staffers by providing members of Congress with the necessary information to write legislation. Second, they relay relevant electoral information to members about the ramifications of legislative proposals on their constituents. Of course, none of this is done altruistically. Lobbying groups are providing this information with the motivation of influencing the content of policy that affects their own interests or furthers their private agendas.

Much of what we know about interest group lobbying seems noncontroversial, even common knowledge. But something clearly has changed. This book uses US agricultural policy as a vehicle to explain how the rapidly polarizing political environment has altered the role of interest groups in Washington. Agricultural policy is one of the most important and appropriate areas of substance for such a book. US agricultural policy impacts the livelihood of millions of people, the success of thousands of companies, and the diet, health, and pocketbooks of hundreds of millions of Americans (and America's trading partners). I argue that polarization has given interest groups greater influence over policy content, particularly with their ideological and partisan allies. Ironically, that same partisan polarization regularly frustrates the capacity of groups to push Washington forward on policy change in a timely fashion, especially in the case of low-salience legislation where bipartisan collaboration matters most. In other words, occasional (perhaps powerful) influence comes at the cost of timely action, or sometimes any action at all. Not only is such bipartisanship in decline, but so is financial investment in congressional capacity for research and fact-finding. Of particular note, Congress's standing committees no longer maintain bipartisan staff, and committee chairs often keep minority party members deliberately in the dark on legislative content (Curry 2015). In response to the changing political climate, I answer the questions: How have interest groups modified their influence-seeking strategies in response to this progressively more polarized political climate and the increasingly hierarchical-information distribution within Congress? And what implications does this have for interest groups' influence on the content of policy?

I answer these questions by looking at lobbying behavior in the agricultural sector over two decades. In order to identify changes in lobbying behavior over time, the book relies on a combination of qualitative and quantitative research approaches. I use elite interviews combined with statistical analysis of an original dataset of interest groups lobbying in the agriculture sector (details about which can be found in the appendices). In doing so, the multimethod approach tells a story about agricultural policy, lobbying, and partisan polarization in Congress. The interviews, in particular, offer insight into the changing political climate within which interest groups operate. This book tells a story of a political environment rife with partisan conflict that has deteriorated communication and trust, particularly worsening after the 2010 midterm elections. I conducted interviews in March 2014, and again in April 2018, and in the years between these two trips the environment continued to shift dramatically in the direction of conflict and suspicion, often described in the stories that follow. Particularly illustrative of this shift is the fact that while a few interviewees in 2014 agreed to allow their names to appear in my work, almost none agreed to allow their name to be used by 2018. In this book you will notice that I therefore anonymize the vast majority of the interviewees. The changing attitude of lobbyists, becoming more cautious and worried about repercussions, seems reflective of the broader environment on Capitol Hill that is increasingly hostile. What role do interest groups have in this brave new world?

At one time, researchers viewed lobbyists as purveyors of information rather than as "pressure" groups; the prevailing idea was that groups were essentially doing a job that could easily be done by congressional staffers and that they wielded relatively little power over actual policy outcomes (Bauer, Pool, and Dexter 1963). But the idea that groups are weak, unorganized, and ineffective at persuading Congress was challenged even at that time (Lowi 1969). One challenge to understanding when and how lobbying mattered was the lack of reliable measures of lobbying and policy outcomes; in fact, a meta-analysis of the literature shows that in 1998, over half of the published studies of lobbying did not contain a direct measure of lobbying (Baumgartner and Leech 1998). Since then, fortunately, the Lobbying Disclosure Act has created a reliable database of lobbying activity at the federal level, on which this book leans heavily. However, statistical analysis can take us only so far because it fails to explain the "why" of behavior. The interviews highlighted in this book add insight from lobbyists and show how these actors perceive their own role in the policymaking system. Together, these approaches reveal a more detailed picture of how lobbyists have adjusted to the massive shifts in partisan politics since the 1990s. In tandem, the interviews and statistical evidence also expand our understanding of the role that lobbying plays in creating policy.

Farmed Out is expansive in turning attention to the substantive impacts that polarization has on policy development. Specifically, the book demonstrates how party polarization expands and alters the role that interest groups play in policy construction and the negotiation process. This expanded view regarding the roll of lobbying in policymaking is a step forward, growing from existing studies concerned with polarization and gridlock, and with lobbying as a form of *political insurance*. It illustrates that interest groups have adapted their strategies and, consequently, have become even more powerful in their influence. *Farmed Out* points to the importance of behind-the-scenes coalition building in the policy process and how these often-unnoticed processes shape public policy for better or worse.

THE PLAN OF THE BOOK

Chapter 2 provides a (very) brief overview of the history of agricultural politics and its place in American politics. This chapter situates agricultural policymaking as a subsystem that has grown and changed over time and, particularly, has expanded drastically to include increasingly more interests as well as more and further-reaching issue areas. The chapter highlights the early days of agricultural policymaking as a temporary crisis response and follows the policy area through large scale readjustments that brought us to the modern food policy regime. These early days created structures that were intended to be temporary, but instead became foundational to American food policy as we now experience it.

Chapter 3 lays out the foundation for understanding the evolving and pivotal role of interest groups in the policymaking process. This chapter details the current nature of the agricultural subsystem, explains how polarization is altering the political landscape, and suggests hypotheses for how lobbying organizations have adapted. Political polarization and gridlock in Congress have led to a fractionated policy process in which even the smallest and seemingly most innocuous pieces of legislation are held up and hotly debated. In this environment, interest groups have become nonpartisan negotiators that often specialize in coalition-building as a tactic to mediate between legislators (and their staffs) who are barely civil to members of the other party. This theory suggests that, with increasing frequency, coalition building occurs external to Congress, not within it. More than ever before, interest groups are doing the work of finding, building, and negotiating coalitions around policy as legislators are increasingly at odds over partisanship and ideological splits on nearly every issue. The days of the lone wolf interest group are over; in interviews, many lobbyists emphasized that interest groups seldom find success alone. Instead, they experience greater success through coalition building and maintenance. This chapter builds a case that, as the institutional capacity of legislative offices and committees has declined, interest groups increasingly take on the coalitional work previously performed in the halls of Congress. This theory moves beyond the traditional view of interest groups as providing informational subsidies and expands their roles into providing *legislative work subsidies*, such as coalition building and negotiating.

Chapter 4 uses corporate lobbying behavior in the agricultural sector as a case study. Even as corporations are some of the most vilified actors in politics, they also are the most active in lobbying. Their motivation is plainly profit, and their preferences are often transparent. Additionally, a fair amount of information about corporations is publicly available in various datasets, allowing for more detailed analysis than is possible with other types of groups, for which there are very little public data. Chapter 4 looks for consistent changes, over time, in corporate lobbying behavior and begins to lay out a case for the motivation behind those changes. This chapter uses a dataset that combines Lobbying Disclosure Act data on lobbying interest groups with data on corporate location and profits from the WRDS Compustat North America (via Wharton) database. I find that the increase in polarization over the past twenty years has had a profound effect on corporate lobbying behavior. Corporate lobbying of Congress has increased even as corporate lobbying levels have remained fairly steady in other venues (such as bureaucratic agencies and executive agencies like the Office of Management and Budget). When this information is combined with evidence from interviews, we can clearly see that polarization in Congress is having a large and important effect on lobbying behavior for firms and other advocacy organizations. Interest groups appear to be working harder (in the form of lobbying Congress) to achieve their preferred outcomes.

Chapter 5 expands the narrative to the advocacy behavior of all interest groups in the agricultural sector and further establishes the role of partisan polarization in increasing lobbying efforts over time, largely due to the more contentious, slow, and gridlocked nature of policymaking. This chapter, like Chapter 4, uses an original dataset, created by combining Lobbying Disclosure Act data on lobbying interest groups with data on political environment and polarization. I find that the increase in polarization over the past twenty years has had a large effect on lobbying behavior, specifically, increasing the amount of effort that interest groups must expend in Congress. The findings are backed by evidence obtained from a series of interviews in which lobbyists express clear awareness of and strategic response to party polarization, utilizing tactics such as providing information, facilitating communication and coordination among members, and building coalitions across the partisan aisle. Overall, it is clear that polarization has an important effect on lobbying strategies, from changing the sheer quantity of lobbying in Congress to altering the techniques that interest groups find to be most successful for achieving their preferred policy outcomes.

Chapter 6 relies on insight from elite interviews to illustrate how polarization has driven real changes in lobbying behavior and has subtly shifted the role of advocacy groups in American politics. Interview subjects described the agricultural policy arena as a unique example of cooperation, negotiation, and good policy process, yet in the same breath noted the way that polarization and uncertainty are impacting the political landscape. Many bemoaned what they saw as the fading bipartisanship of days gone by and described a world in which interest groups were asked to choose sides in the escalating battle between parties in Congress. Most importantly, this chapter describes how escalating partisan tensions have transformed the lobbying industry and the roles that lobbyists must take up. Recent evidence suggests that, both through a decline in overall institutional capacity and through deliberate leadership action, rank and file members of Congress have ever less information and less influence over the content of legislation (Curry 2015). Lobbyists, increasingly, are stepping in to fill this void. While lobbyists have always provided informational subsidies to legislators (Hall and Deardorff 2006), their role has morphed to include a *negotiation subsidy*. As members of Congress, and particularly the House, have become less collegial, lobbyists work harder to act as go-betweens and negotiators. They form industry coalitions that appeal across the partisan aisle, and in doing so, they provide political cover for members of Congress to support emerging compromises. Indeed, coalition building was described to take up an increasing amount of time for lobbyists, and to be increasingly vital to their success. As one interviewee put it, "the days of the lone voice are over."[1] These coalitions also provide the groups with political cover; in a coalition they are less likely to be pressed to affiliate with one partisan side or another. In short, partisanship is not only increasing the amount of lobbying on Capitol Hill, it is also changing its form. As the political landscape has shifted, interest groups have adapted.

Chapter 7 considers the implications of increased informational and negotiation subsidies from interest groups on policy outcomes. In particular, it probes the trade-off for many interest groups between increased influence over policy, at the cost of more expensive advocacy, and less timely congressional action. While high-salience, must-pass legislation, like the farm bill, often makes it through the legislative process, albeit with much conflict and angst, lower salience legislation that was once comparatively easy to pass is more often a casualty of a gridlocked and bitterly partisan process. This chapter highlights the consequences of this tradeoff: a widening divide between "rich" and "poor" interest groups in terms of their influence and success in the system. As we will find, relatively poorer groups lobby less than richer groups and are less likely to have in-house lobbyists to do the work. This suggests that being wealthier means getting a bigger "bang for your [lobbying] buck," so to speak. Wealthier groups are able to hire more long-term lobbyists, and therefore, in the long run, engage in more successful advocacy. This is, perhaps, not a new phenomenon. But it is an increasingly important phenomenon as the legislative timeline stretches longer and longer from ideation to execution.

Chapter 8 summarizes the key insights: party polarization, combined with reduced congressional capacity for information gathering, has resulted in an increase in lobbying toward Congress. Interest groups now provide not only informational subsidies but also negotiation subsidies for members and their staffs. The expanded role for lobbyists in policy making, combined with the increasingly fraught political environment in Washington, has broadened the "gulf of influence" between rich and poor interest groups and their ability to take a seat at the table, with implications for interest group advocacy broadly, as well as for agricultural policy specifically. This chapter concludes with a discussion of the possible substantive policy implications resulting from the shifts in interest group strategy and power. Even as consumers demand more "family farms," "sustainable agriculture," and "organic" products, the kinds of groups with sway in Washington are ever less reflective of the spirit of these consumer demands. Lobbying has always favored the rich, powerful, and strong; it does so now more than ever.

While this book digs into the making of food and agriculture policy, it offers insights that are applicable more broadly. Beyond the agricultural subsystem, Congress more broadly has changed dramatically over the past two decades, with rapid partisan polarization, more demanding electoral politics, fewer nonpartisan staff, and increasingly technically complex regulatory challenges (social media, privacy in an era of connectedness, financial regulations from subprime mortgages to bitcoin, and more). These changes create new dynamics for policymaking. Interest groups and corporations may find themselves providing more information to Congress, being called upon to testify more frequently, and becoming ever more involved in politics (Drutman 2015), while the actual work of passing laws seems to occur at barely a snail's pace, if at all. Who wins, who loses, and who has a voice is changing.

2

A Growing Policy Area

The Creation of Agriculture as a
Staple of American Politics

To tell a story about how lobbying is changing in the current congressional environment, this book focuses on one policy area in particular: food and agriculture. American agricultural policy is, arguably, one of the most underrated and publicly under-attended-to issues; the food and agriculture policy decisions made in the halls of Congress touch the daily lives of every American, and much of the rest of the globe as well, affecting our pocketbooks, waistlines, community cultures, environment, and so much more.

Food and agriculture policy does not *only* encompass the farm bill; and yet, when we talk about food and agriculture policy in the United States, the conversation is inevitably, and correctly, dominated by the farm bill. This omnibus legislation (typically a large bill including nearly any and every relevant piece of public policy) is passed approximately every five years and establishes the basic contours of agriculture, nutrition, and conservation policy nationwide, and its policies affect global markets and food prices and access worldwide.

The farm bill consists of twelve titles, in total. These are: commodity programs, conservation, trade, nutrition programs, credit, rural development, research and related matters, forestry, energy, horticulture, crop

---

Farmed Out. Clare R. Brock, Oxford University Press. © Clare R. Brock 2024.
DOI: 10.1093/oso/9780197683798.003.0002

insurance, and miscellaneous. Of these titles, just five comprise the vast majority of spending. The 2018 farm bill projected a total outlay of $428 billion over five years. In that bill, the nutrition title accounts for 76.1% of all spending, crop insurance is 8.9%, commodities accounts for 7.3%, and conservation accounts for 6.8% of spending; the other titles, together, receive the remaining 0.8% of funding ("Farm Bill Spending" 2022). And importantly, this spending structure represents very little departure from the status quo of other farm bills in the recent past.

However, the broad contours of food and agriculture policy are set through other legislation as well. The Healthy, Hunger-Free Kids Act of 2010 and the Food Safety and Modernization Act are two particularly notable, recent examples. Coronavirus relief packages, too, contained provisions that touched on food and agriculture policy, including funds intended to help farmers and producers nationwide.

Beyond the reach that food and agriculture policy have in impacting the day-to-day lives of Americans, this policy area is substantively important for understanding interest group influence and behavior. Farm policy was one of the earliest areas for interest group influence in Congress, and as the policy area has expanded, so too have the number and diversity of interests weighing in on the legislative process. This introductory chapter outlines some of the major historical moments and trends in American food policy which have led us to the current policy environment in which this book is set, before proceeding to the main argument of the book.

THE INVENTION OF THE FARM BILL

The early 1900s, until Franklin Roosevelt's election in 1932, was an era of "small government"; yet, in the years leading up to the 1933 farm bill, Congress began to intervene in the agricultural marketplace with price-fixing measures, as "lawmakers opened their deliberations to the farm lobby" (Hansen 1991, 27). These early interventions set the stage for the more significant interventions to come. When the southern agricultural economy (cotton in particular) collapsed almost entirely in 1930 and

1931, the economic devastation created massive mobilization for farm relief throughout the entirety of the South (Hansen 1991). It was during these early months of the Great Depression that the first-ever farm bill was constructed and the Agricultural Adjustment Act (AAA) of 1933 was signed into law as part of the New Deal. This first farm bill was largely oriented around reducing surplus and raising crop prices, while later farm bills addressed soil erosion and added various programs to support farmers, including establishing the Federal Crop Insurance Corporation in 1938 (Devarenne and DeSimone n.d.).

The AAA of 1933, then, was a response to crisis, a result of "the trauma experienced by the nation's farm communities in the late 1920s and early 1930s, depicted in searing photographic images of the Dust Bowl and rural poverty" (Bosso 2017, 35). In a sense, the AAA of 1933, and its early descendants, were actually *conservation* bills. They were intended to encourage farmers to reduce the acreage they were farming and start implementing conservation techniques. The early farm bills were also oriented around reducing farm outputs, rather than ramping up production. Such policy decisions might seem counterintuitive from a modern perspective; but, during this time, farmers were going bankrupt and leaving their farms at an alarming rate due to low commodity prices—they were caught in the collective trap of growing an oversupply of food (often using unsustainable farming practices), thereby flooding the market and lowering prices, which then incentivized the farmers to grow even more in attempt to earn more money, and so on, ad infinitum—so limiting supply was a strategic move to try to force farmers into more sustainable planting and production practices while simultaneously increasing potential profits. As government policy began to affect farmers, there emerged a need for farmers to organize and lobby in effort to influence this policy. By 1932, a Washington reporter wrote that the farm lobby was "the most powerful single-industry lobby in Washington" (Hansen 1991, 75).

As agricultural techniques and advocacy were evolving, so was public attention to nutrition; the 1920s and 1930s were a time of new interest in nutrition and health in America, particularly in response to the Great

Depression. Public attention focused on questions of malnutrition, and people were particularly concerned with the impact that lack of food might have on children's development. "Hot lunch clubs," funded by parents or by parent-teacher fundraisers, began to pop up in lunchrooms around the country, and many state Agricultural Extension Service Offices ran school lunch programs or developed nutrition education materials to be used by home economics teachers (Levine 2008, 37). However, these lunch programs were largely ad hoc and underfunded. When the New Deal began to expand the role of federal government in the 1930s, new opportunities opened for nutrition advocates to put healthy food in cafeterias across the country.

In 1946, the first National School Lunch program (NSLP) was created. However, this program was not, at its heart, a nutrition program, it was an agricultural program. In spite of being authorized separately from the farm bill, the program was organized as a commodity disposal program for surplus foods and was run through the US Department of Agriculture; the program was also specifically restricted to students who could not pay for school meals (Levine 2008). One crucial reason that the NSLP was restricted to students whose families could not afford to purchase food was that congressional and administrative interests were still dominated by southern Democratic legislators who generally opposed federal social programs (Levine 2008) but were closely connected to the Farm Bureau, which held powerful influence and arguably had the power to control a majority of votes in both the House and the Senate (Hansen 1991). Using the NSLP as a commodity dumping program neatly solved the problem of surplus agricultural products while also addressing the public outcry about malnutrition and hunger nationwide. The program operated this way until the NSLP was threatened with dissolution in 1943.

In 1943, President Roosevelt shifted responsibility for the NSLP to the new War Food Administration (WFA), which drastically expanded the program for the duration of World War II in an effort to ensure that young men were prepared for war. At Roosevelt's White House National Nutrition Conference for Defense, Surgeon General Thomas Parran argued that:

Forty percent of the American population are not properly fed. The ill-health results mean a slowing down of industrial production, a danger to military strength, and a lowering of the morale of millions. ... I hope that this Conference will make recommendations to solve nutrition problems at national, State, and community levels as an essential part of defense and as a part of a continuing national health and welfare program. (*Proceedings of the National Nutrition Conference for Defense 1942*, VIII)

In other words, the NSLP began as a commodity dumping program and was later framed as a matter of national security and military preparedness. After the war, with the program's codification into new federal legislation, the 1946 National School Lunch Act declared the policy to be "a measure of national security, to safeguard the health and well-being of the Nation's children and to encourage the domestic consumption of nutritious agricultural commodities." (Gunderson 2003, 30). In this spirit, the program was transferred back to the USDA. In short, while the NSLP is not administered through the farm bill, it was and is still inextricably connected to farm interests and is effectively used as a subsidy for farmers, rather than as a health and nutrition program in its own right. Since its inception, the program has had the dual purpose of feeding children while boosting the American agricultural economy.

COLD WAR, BIG AG

It wasn't until 1973 that anti-hunger programs and the farm bill became formally connected. Indeed, current farm and food policy has its roots in the farm bills of the 1970s and 1980s. While the earliest farm bills focused on limiting farm production, it was during the Cold War years that US agricultural policy underwent a fundamental shift, setting a new precedent for the policies that are now status quo. During the 1950s and 1960s, US agricultural production boomed. Hoping to offload some of the surplus and improve international relations, the Nixon administration sold stockpiles of feed corn and wheat to the Soviet Union. Unfortunately, an unexpected drought hit the Grain Belt of the Midwest in 1976, and global food market prices began to increase, infuriating American consumers (Bosso 2017, 39). In effort to ease grain prices, Earl Butz, Nixon's secretary of agriculture, encouraged American farmers to plant "fencerow to fencerow" (Risser and Anthan 1976) and used the 1973 Agriculture and Consumer Protection Act to reorient farm policy around maximizing production (Bosso 2017, 39). To incentivize farmers to maximize production, the new policy created direct payments to farmers whenever market prices fell below target prices.

Convincing Congress to make direct commodity payments to farmers, however, was challenging. By the 1970s, agricultural organizations represented increasingly fewer voters as people migrated away from farms and toward urban centers; to boost their leverage in Congress, rural representatives cut deals with consumer and hunger advocates to include food stamps in the farm bill for the first time (Hansen 1991, 111). The food stamp program was formally created by the Food Stamp Act of 1964, though it had previously been run (from 1961 through 1964) as a pilot program ("A Short History of SNAP" 2018). But in 1973, the program was formally rolled into the farm bill and expanded drastically, both in participant eligibility and in funds available to provide recipients with a "nutritionally adequate diet" ("A Short History of SNAP" 2018). While nutrition programs had been used as outlets for agricultural surplus previously, this incorporation created the first formal, and now longstanding, link between nutrition and agriculture policy in the United States.

Later reauthorizations of the farm bill created conservation programs and incentives, but the new commodity subsidy policy remained the underpinning of the legislation (Bosso 2017), encouraging large-scale, "fencerow to fencerow" planting practices. The 1985 farm bill created, for the first time, a formal conservation title that created the Conservation Reserve Program (CRP) and the Wetlands Reserve Program (WRP). Subsequent farm bills slowly added additional programs, such as the Environmental Quality Incentives Program (EQIP), the Wildlife Habitat Incentives Program (WHIP), and the Conservation Security Program

(CSP). These programs were, and are, voluntary programs that farmers may enter to receive payments for planting native flora on vulnerable lands, create buffer zones between their planting and eligible wetlands, and receive financial assistance and cost sharing for implementing conservation practices.

Expanding the omnibus nature of the farm bill, and bringing a new, wider set of interests into the legislation—nutrition and conservation interests in particular—has offered the farm bill some protection and a base of stakeholders even as the number of actual farmers in America has dwindled. However, a wider array of involved interests has not prevented the creep of partisanship into the policy area.

FREEDOM FARMING

In the mid-1990s, lawmakers were ready to undertake another massive shift to US agricultural policy. From the 96th Congress (1979–1980) until Newt Gingrich rose to the Speaker's rostrum in the 104th Congress (1995–1996), Republicans in the House become steadily more conservative with each class that entered the chamber (Theriault 2013, 28). It was in this atmosphere, with Republicans controlling both chambers of Congress and Gingrich at the helm of the House, that lawmakers passed the Federal Agriculture Improvement and Reform Act (FAIR Act, also known as the Freedom to Farm Bill) (PL 104-127). The FAIR Act aimed to eliminate most supply controls, phase out government subsidies for crops, eliminate direct government purchases of dairy products, and generally encourage farmers to meet market demand without government interference (Nelson and Schertz 1996). It was in this bill that the new House Speaker, Newt Gingrich (R-GA), first pushed to split food stamps out of the farm bill as part of the "Contract with America"; however, he was persuaded against doing so by Pat Roberts (R-KS), who was the House Agriculture Committee chair at the time (Bosso 2017, 62). House Republicans also wanted to fully repeal the permanent law contained in the Agricultural Act of 1949, but Senate Democrats, backed by a credible veto threat from

President Bill Clinton, refused, on the logic that the permanent law was "rural America's guarantee that Congress would revisit farm policy on a regular basis" (Bosso 2017, 43). Democrats opposed large portions of the bill, with David Obey (D-WI) saying during floor debate, "This is probably the worst farm bill to have hit the floor of the House in the last 25 years" (*Congressional Record* 1996). It is worth noting that, after retirement in January of 2011, Obey moved to Gephardt Government Affairs, where he would lobby with his former colleague Dick Gephardt (Frates 2011).

The FAIR Act was intended to expire after seven years but was quickly and obviously a disastrous policy failure. While the act was popular with farmers initially, who were convinced that they could "out compete any farmer in the world," attitudes soured quickly and the legislation was soon referred to among farmers as the "Freedom to Fail Act" (Schaffer and Ray 2018). As agricultural production increased, global commodity prices deceased correspondingly. The combination ultimately ended up leaving farmers worse off than they would have been under the previous policy structure (Doering and Paarlberg 1999). For the next four years, Congress authorized emergency payments, effectively returning to the status quo, and entirely undermining the intentions behind the FAIR Act. And in 2002, Congress passed a new farm bill, two years before the intended expiration of the Freedom to Farm Act, with the intent to stabilize farm policy and end reliance on emergency payments (Schaffer and Ray 2018).

LOBBYING AND AGRICULTURE

It is during the post–FAIR Act years that the analysis for this book begins. In an ideal world, comparing the lobbying environment of the early 1990s, leading up to the passage of the FAIR Act, to lobbying in the late 1990s and the subsequent years would be highly instructive. However, the Lobbying Disclosure Act (LDA) did not exist yet (it went into effect in 1998), and we therefore have no formal records or data regarding lobbying during these years. Instead, this book begins with the introduction of the LDA and continues through just before passage of the 2014 farm bill. In doing so, the book explores some of the significant legislation and important environmental changes in the food and agriculture policy and advocacy space in the sixteen years after the LDA went into effect.

Indeed, the late 1990s and early 2000s are an ideal time period to explore in the study of the changing advocacy landscape in agriculture, because these years represent a shift in the structural and political environment of the institution. These changes are discussed at length in the chapters that follow. Some of the broad policies that were enacted during this time include:

Public Health Security and Bioterrorism Preparedness and Response Act of 2002. This act aimed at improving the country's defenses against potential bioterrorist acts and ensuring the integrity of the national food system.

Farm Security and Rural Investment Act of 2002. This farm bill included controversial country-of-origin labeling (COOL) requirements for certain foods including lamb, goat, and chicken, some nuts, and certain fish.

Food Allergy Labeling and Consumer Protection Act of 2004. This act requires labeling of foods that potentially contain or are derived from peanuts, soybeans, cow's milk, eggs, fish, shellfish, tree nuts, and wheat.

Food, Conservation, and Energy Act of 2008. This farm bill significantly increased funding for the Food Stamp Program (to be renamed the Supplemental Nutrition Assistance Program) and was passed by a Democratic Congress, vetoed by President George W. Bush, and passed again in a rare veto-override.

Healthy, Hunger-Free Kids Act of 2010. This legislation updated the nutrition standards for school lunches and included provisions aimed at encouraging more farm-to-school programs, reducing unhealthy beverages in school vending machines, and improving lunch programs for schools with high proportions of low-income students, in particular.

Food Safety and Modernization Act of 2010. Aimed at updating food safety laws and improve the tracking and tracing of food and foodborne illnesses. This law included provisions for additional food inspection, testing, and a new mandatory recall program.

Agricultural Act of 2014. This farm bill, at one time titled the Federal Agriculture Reform and Risk Management Act, contained significant cuts to nutrition titles, which caused Democrats to oppose it, but insufficient cuts to attract the support of Tea Party Republicans, who joined House Democrats in defeating the bill on the House floor in 2013—an unprecedented outcome for a farm bill vote. This caused delays which ultimately meant the bill was not signed into law by President Obama until early 2014.

The specific stories of some of these bills are told in the chapters that follow, while others are not, but all of this policymaking happens in the context of what scholars consider the agricultural policymaking subsystem. In other words, food and agriculture policy extends beyond the farm bill, though the farm bill remains the centerpiece of the policy arena—also known as a subsystem.

SUBSYSTEM POLITICS: WHO IS IN AND WHO IS OUT?

The study of interest group influence begins generally with the principle that subsystems are the informal micro-institutions in which lobbying occurs. Once known as "iron triangles," they consist of committees, interest groups, and bureaucracies who, together, make policy-relevant decisions. These subsystems form and reform as policy ideas come and go, attracting different players and interests with each new policy idea. While the core elements may remain, the coalitions and players can shift.

One key question that political scientists have discussed is how open subsystems are to new "players." In other words, when new policy ideas emerge on the agenda, are new participants able to enter the subsystem and influence the decision-making process?

Some scholars have found relatively closed or captured subsystems, indicating a high level of access and influence for a few interest groups, and low access for others (Hansen 1991; Worsham 2006). In this scenario, some interest groups have high levels of influence because they have gained the trust of lawmakers who are in positions of leadership and power. This theoretically privileges interest groups who have lobbied repeatedly over the years (they have staying power) and have built a reputation for speaking accurately regarding the preferences of their members. These groups also wield influence because of the relative power they have to create electoral consequences for members of Congress who defy their interests.

However, other scholars have found open and fluid subsystems or even relatively autonomous government actors, indicating a lower level of access or influence for any one interest group, but also the allowance for many to impact the policy process in smaller ways (Browne 1988; Finegold 1995; Gais, Peterson, and Walker 1984; A. D. Sheingate 2003). In the scenario of a more open subsystem, interest groups tend to wield influence in their niche areas, often avoiding conflict with other interest groups and exclusively lobbying on a very specific issue. This allows interest groups to lobby only on those issues that directly influence their bottom line or their members, and avoid broader political fights, particularly ones that may hinge on ideological conflicts rather than material benefits for the interest group. In debating the nature of modern subsystems, scholars have often used agriculture policy as a case study in their research, but there is no consensus on which kind of subsystem agricultural policy falls into. The lack of consensus, perhaps, indicates that subsystems can be either open or closed, depending on which issues are being considered and how entrenched those issues are. How open or closed a subsystem is can vary over time, or by the specific issue that is being considered—in other words, there is not a clear or concrete answer to whether or not a subsystem is officially "open" or "closed," and there does not need to be—openness and closedness exist on a continuum and vary across time and issue.

At any degree of relative openness or closedness, the agricultural subsystem has historically been an unusually bipartisan policy area. This does not mean *consensual*, to be clear. Rather, agriculture policy has historically tended to be characterized by regional cleavages—what is good for pig farmers is not necessarily what is good for grain farmers or dairy farmers and is certainly not aligned with the interests of tomato growers or sugar cane producers. However, the subsystem is now in a moment of flux, as the stories in this book illustrate, and legislation being drafted within the subsystem (particularly the farm bill) is increasingly contentious (Sheingate 2013). Polarization theoretically creates an environment in which we should expect subsystem reformation and, accordingly, behavior change on the part of interest groups; yet we have only weak theories for *how* polarization should change lobbying behavior. The following chapters consider how partisan polarization is serving to reform agricultural policymaking and the new coalitions that might form as a result.

3

Work Hard for the Money

Polarization and Evolving Lobbying Strategies

*Farm policy, we've regarded as the last bastion of bipartisanship, and
we've been grateful for that. But right now, we're really worried. . . .
House polarization is rearing its ugly head for us right now.*[1]

In examining the effect of partisan polarization on interest group
lobbying in agricultural policymaking, *polarization* can be understood
to mean "an expansion of the distance between the issue positions of
Democrats and Republicans" (Mason 2018, 17). As the previous chapters
discussed, the American food and agriculture subsystem is in the midst
of a partisan breakdown. Members of Congress, particularly in the
House, arrive with increasingly conservative or liberal policy positions.
As a consequence, partisan and ideological conflict over the contents of
the farm bill, and nearly every other piece of legislation proposed, is at
a new high.

Partisan polarization in Congress has resulted in increased conflict
(Theriault 2013) and has coincided with increased time and information
pressures on its members. Time spent campaigning, dialing for dollars,
and visiting the home district all have steadily increased in recent years,

Farmed Out. Clare R. Brock, Oxford University Press. © Clare R. Brock 2024.
DOI: 10.1093/oso/9780197683798.003.0003

and cumulatively represents time that cannot be spent on legislative activities (Beckel 2017; Klein 2013). At the same time, they work with less staff support; the numbers of staffers employed in the House and Senate committees, and by support agencies like the Congressional Research Service, have steadily declined since the 1980s (Vital Statistics on Congress 2021). As a result, members of Congress increasingly turn to lobbyists to provide policy expertise and research—essentially, to act as adjunct staffers (Boehmke, Gailmard, and Patty 2013; Hall and Deardorff 2006; LaPira and Thomas 2017). In a legislative environment in which members' schedules are overloaded and committees are understaffed, *credible* information is valuable, but it is also unevenly distributed. Congressional leadership increasingly uses information restriction as a tool for partisan control (Curry 2015). It is not that members of Congress lack information, per se; it is that they lack the *correct* information at the correct time, in no small part because their leaders now often fail to provide the text of important legislation until the day before a vote; this restriction operates both as a means of forcing rank-and-file members to rely on cues from leadership to make decisions, and as a way to deprive the opposition of any fodder for a well-constructed or specific attack on the substance of proposed legislation (Curry 2015). As a result, the potential real-world consequences of enacting complex policy may be poorly understood by many, or all, of the policymakers involved, with members of Congress more eager to better understand the electoral ramifications of their votes on particular policies, possibly even more concerned with electoral than substantive outcomes at particular times or on particular issues.

This poverty of *correct* information, coupled with an overabundance of unwinnowed information among rank-and-file members of Congress changes how interest groups influence policymaking. Hansen argues that "lobbies achieve influence in Congress to the degree that legislators choose their counsel, to the degree that legislators grant them access" (1991, 2). And yet, in recent years, interactions are changing both in terms of how interest groups interact with members of Congress and in terms of how they interact with other interest groups. Worse, the attentive public now assumes that interactions between lobbyists and legislators are necessarily corrupt—a trade of money for policy—even if scholars are less certain about such popular wisdom. That disjuncture has implications for the already frayed legitimacy of our governing institutions.

THE INFORMATIONAL SUBSIDY

Research investigating the potential quid pro quo relationship between organized interests and politicians often looks to campaign contributions to measure influence. The study of money in politics, broadly speaking, begins with the assumption that groups want their preferences to be codified into law, where possible. There are many ways that organized interests can achieve their desired outcomes: means such as media outreach, litigation, illegal activities (acting on firm preferences in conflict with the law might occur when penalties are small but payoffs are large), making campaign contributions (potentially resulting in quid pro quo exchanges between interests and lawmakers), and lobbying directed at either Congress or the bureaucracy. However, not all these behaviors are equal in their potential payoffs. For example, litigation carries the risk that existing law might not be interpreted in a group's interests. Free media can be unpredictable, and it leaves an interest group or company with very little control over how it is represented. Illegal activity, such as running a slaughter line at a faster-than-legal speed, could lead to negative public opinion or legal consequences, creating unforeseen costs that exceed the payoffs. Further, each behavior has heavy costs (paying public relations firms, hiring lawyers, organizing politically, etc.), meaning that groups must calculate the relative trade-offs and benefits gained from each path. Presumably, having one's preferences represented in the body of law is the maximum payoff for any interest, though this does not mean that all interest groups will expend the energy to gain this benefit. For this reason, if interests do choose to seek representation in the body of law, making campaign contributions on a hypothetically quid pro quo basis or engaging in lobbying would be preferable.

Of course, quid pro quo exchanges are illegal. And the findings regarding such trade-offs between members of Congress and organized interests suggest that the exchange is very subtle, and that campaign contributions do not necessarily lead to favorable legislative outputs (Hall and Wayman 1990; Milyo, Primo, and Groseclose 2000; Welch 1982). While one 1982 study on the legislation of milk subsidies found a direct connection between campaign contributions and congressional behavior, it also found that members of Congress were rewarded *after* a favorable vote rather than before (Welch 1982). What can be said with certainty is that campaign contributions motivate members to spend more time on an issue (Hall and Wayman 1990). Overall, the evidence does not suggest that interest groups can rely on campaign contributions to obtain favorable legislative outcomes.

However, that interests are not "buying votes" does not equate to a lack of influence. Money has other ways of making a difference. It can help just to get in the door, so to speak. One analysis shows that committee-level voting by members of the House Agriculture or Ways and Means Committees is best explained by the number of contacts the members received (and therefore the amount of spending targeted in their direction) from groups on each side of an issue (Wright 1990). And others have demonstrated that among foreign lobbyists, for whom we have more information regarding specific lobbying contacts, it is common to request access to legislators to whom they have made a campaign contribution (Liu 2021). There is also some evidence that lobbyists who host fundraisers for legislators are more likely to see favorable amendments added to legislation (McKay 2019). But, even here, researchers have a hard time establishing causal linkages with explicit legislative *outcomes* (after all, offering an amendment does not guarantee success). For example, some research has attempted to draw parallels between lobbying expenditures and political action committee (PAC) campaign contributions, but this research has resulted in different conclusions. If one study concludes that because lobbying expenditures mirror PAC campaign contribution expenditures, which have been found to have no effect, lobbying must not affect policy outcomes (Milyo, Primo, and Groseclose 2000), another finds that PAC contributions, and thus lobbying, are influential in congressional decision making (Langbein 1993).

But such studies, comparing the success of campaign contributions to the success of lobbying efforts, often suffer from methodological problems, among them a failure to account for issue-related characteristics or to directly measure lobbying (Baumgartner and Leech 1998). Many of these studies conflate lobbying expenditures and campaign contributions, which are entirely distinct activities; lobbying involves no direct transfer of capital between interests and members of Congress (de Figueiredo 2002). Importantly, interest groups who lobby, and those who contribute to campaigns, are not always the same, though there is certainly overlap; and among those who do contribute, they often contribute much less than is allowed to PACs, who spend much less than the maximum in making contributions (Ansolabehere, de Figueiredo, and Snyder 2003). The choice not to be involved in campaigns is often a deliberate one for lobbying groups. One lobbyist explained:

> We don't engage in electoral politics at all. We don't contribute to campaigns, we don't have a PAC, so we basically don't have money. But we have lots and lots of members. We have 106 member organizations; some of them are small and some are huge, so there's millions of potential constituents there. So that's what we are best known [for], both for our legislative and campaign development work in DC, and then also for having the troops that we can mobilize. People know they're going to hear from us. And Capitol Hill offices occasionally call and say, "Okay we got the message, tell them to stop calling us!" But we don't play in the campaign finance game at all. So, we're not in that neck of the woods. And we don't litigate.[2]

Even among those interest groups that do make campaign contributions, they tend to do so at a relatively modest level—campaign contribution spending is much less than we would expect, if we believed that campaigns bought political outcomes (Ansolabehere, de Figueiredo, and Snyder 2003). Another lobbyist explained it in the following way: "With a PAC, which is normally what companies deal with—PACs—it's pretty limited, right? So, you can give ten thousand dollars to somebody who is running a Senate campaign that's ten million dollars." Indeed, 2020 was the most expensive election yet in American history, with the Biden campaign raising over $1 billion in donations and the Trump campaign raising $774 million, with a large portion of those contributions coming from small donors (Evers-Hillstrom 2021). Those numbers sound impressive, but consider that in that same year Americans spent $889.3 billion on their Christmas shopping (Holmes 2022). In other words, holiday shopping dwarfs political spending 800:1. If campaign contributions bought policy outcomes, one can only imagine that corporate America would go policy shopping more often and with a bigger budget. And yet, concluding that lobbying must not be effective because there is not a clear effect from campaign contributions counters intuition as well as evidence from other fields.

Lobbying can instead be defined relatively broadly as an attempt to persuade or encourage legislators (Denzau and Munger 1986; Hall and Wayman 1990; Hojnacki and Kimball 1998). To be clear, these persuasive efforts are not confined to persuasion on final votes; in fact, very little of lobbying is focused on changing final vote outcomes. A lobbyist would need to persuade a legislator to potentially overlook his or her personal preferences, as well as potentially overlook the preferences of his or her constituency, in order to change a "no" vote to a "yes." Further, looking at votes alone disguises the "sausage-making" process where essential policy details are negotiated (Baumgartner and Leech 1998). By providing information (both policy and political), rather than buying votes, lobbyists are in the potentially powerful position of participating in the policy construction process, as they attempt to structure the range of policy proposals being considered. Whether or not lobbying should be considered a form of agenda setting is debatable, as it has been argued that lobbyists determine those issues on which they will lobby after the agenda has been set by members of Congress (Baumgartner and Leech 1998). Even so, lobbyists certainly participate in the conversation, and are likely able to at least influence the agenda gradually, if indirectly. Most of all, lobbyists engage primarily in providing information to lawmakers, a behavior that occurs over time and well before voting occurs on the floor. Here, information acquisition is costly to lawmakers either because of scarcity, or, as is increasingly the case, because information is *plentiful*, and winnowing it is highly time-consuming. Information is not provided on a quid pro quo basis; rather, information is provided to assist lawmakers who are in relevant offices or who have similar policy positions to the interested groups. And it is in this sausage-making process where the environment is changing due to major partisan shifts where the real power lies.

Though the public often views campaign contributions as a more "sexy" and powerful source of political influence, lobbying is a multibillion-dollar industry. In fact, it is also possible that many people do not distinguish between campaign contributions and lobbying at all. To many Americans, if not most, money in politics is all the same, no matter the form it takes. However, campaign contributions are related to the attempt to sway election outcomes, while lobbying relates to attempts to sway policy outcomes. Groups may engage in both or only one of these activities, but they are distinct activities. Firms that engage in lobbying often find success in influencing regulation and legislation, and subsequently experience considerable financial gains in the marketplace (Alexander, Mazza, and Scholz 2009; Blau, Brough, and Thomas 2011; Hill, Kelly, Lockhart, and Van Ness 2013; Hochberg, Sapienza, and Vissing-Jørgensen 2009; Mathur and Singh 2011; Mian, Sufi, and Trebbi 2010; Richter 2011; Yu and Yu 2012). One study found that firms engaged in lobbying saw a return of over $220 for every $1 spent on the activity (Alexander, Mazza, and Scholz 2009). Additionally, firms clearly believe that they benefit from lobbying, whether for the purpose of influencing new legislation (comparatively rare), or simply by protecting the stability of the status quo (LaPira and Thomas 2017).

Most policy decision-making in Congress happens in committee. It is in committee where the status quo is protected or shaken, where the devil lurks in the details, and where much of the major change in policy occurs. Congressional committees specialize in information gathering and formulating—and amending—legislation. These committees must identify problems (define the problem space) and propose solutions. The committee system solves several dilemmas for Congress: organizing and winnowing information, enabling credit claiming necessary for reelection, allowing legislators to work on those issues they care most about, and providing particularized benefits. But the ground is shifting beneath the committees. Increasingly, committee leaders, in partnership with partisan leaders, restrict the legislative information flow (Curry 2015). In doing so, they prevent other committee members, especially those in the minority party, from making fully informed decisions regarding whether or not to support proposed legislation (Curry 2015). The reason for this, as you might surmise, is the desire of party leaders to strengthen their control, increase rank-and-file member dependence on direction from leadership, and deprive the opposition of sufficient information to mount a well-informed or targeted campaign against drafted legislation (Curry 2015).

DIGGING INTO AGRICULTURE

However, such information restriction has not occurred in all committees, across all policy areas, uniformly. Food and agriculture, as a policy subsystem—a configuration of informal decision-making arrangements within government that often encompass external interest group representatives—resisted the slide into partisanship long after other policy areas fell victim to it. Such ultra-partisanship was arguably ushered in by Newt Gingrich (R-GA) and the Republican senators who previously served in the House with him and became particularly prevalent during the 1990s and early 2000s (Theriault 2013). However, the agricultural and food policymaking subsystem resisted the gravitational forces of partisanship—forces that pull members inward toward the party—longer than others, in no small part because it encompasses a unique array of cross-cutting interest group coalitions: farmers *and* hunger advocates; nutrition advocates *and* food manufacturers, and so on.[3] These broader coalitions in agricultural policymaking are increasingly critical, as the number of farmers in America has gradually shrunk, meaning that farmers represent an increasingly small voting bloc, even as they continue to represent a critical policy area. And agricultural interest groups are acutely aware of their comparatively small size, yet critical position in the American populace; "When you think U.S. farmers and American farmers we're probably 2 percent of the population of that. And so to advance legislation that is imperative, both for food security in the United States, as well as it's tied directly to national security, [we work in coalitions with others]."[4] This cross-cutting nature of the agricultural subsystem extends to legislator reelection interests too. Legislators from agricultural states find themselves in bed, so to speak, with legislators from states with highly urban populations (Bosso 2017), a marriage of mutual convenience that historically withstood partisan pressures. Consider Democrat George McGovern and Republican Robert Dole, who in 2002 pushed legislation through Congress to establish a permanent international school food program. The McGovern–Dole Program fed millions of children across forty-one countries and served as inspiration for future programs created by the United Nations and other international organizations (2008: Dole and McGovern n.d.). In short, bipartisan coalitions have historically been not only achievable but desirable in the building of food and agriculture policy in the United States.

The formation of these coalitions has to do with the historical relationship between agricultural assistance and hunger relief. In the earliest days of American agricultural policy, these coalitions grew out of a need to find publicly acceptable ways to prop up farmers. During the Great

Depression, agricultural commodity prices were at a devastating low, resulting in a vicious cycle in which farmers dumped increasing volumes of crops and animals into markets with the hope of making a profit, simultaneously further driving commodity prices down. During the early 1930s, the federal government bought surplus commodities to drive prices back up and support the market. Initially the plan was to destroy the surplus crops;[5] however, public outrage over such waste in the midst of a deep depression was swift and brutal. Eventually, as described in Chapter 1, other forms of surplus disposal and diversion were devised, including an early version of a school lunch program that provided surplus food to schoolchildren who would otherwise go hungry (Levine 2008, 46). Critically, the government required that food only be provided to children who would not otherwise have food, so most families were still purchasing lunches for their children, stimulating the economy and keeping farms afloat (Levine 2008). It was in this historical moment that agriculture and anti-hunger advocates began to experience a linked fate that has been replicated and reinforced with each subsequent iteration of the farm bill or modification to nutrition programs, from food stamps to the national school lunch program.

For decades, the farm bill enjoyed relative popularity and a general consensus of support in Congress; these broad, cross-cutting coalitions ensured that members of Congress were able to justify supporting the farm bill regardless of their district characteristics. Much of the conflict over the content of farm bills was less partisan than the result of differences among regional production interests (Hansen 1991). The needs of midwestern corn and beef producers were different from those of southern cotton and peanut farmers, or northern dairy farmers, with farm bills generally reflecting an agreement to compromise in ways that supported all crops and producers.

Today, however, while there is certainly still industry- and sector-based conflict within the agricultural landscape, partisan conflict has slowly but steadily seeped into the agricultural policymaking space, mirroring the broader congressional climate. A large portion of this conflict centers on conservative Republican efforts to break hunger and nutrition legislation away from the farm bill so that these programs can be dismantled (Campiche and Sanders 2017). Comparing the 2008 farm bill process to the 2013 process illustrates this break clearly.

As the GOP has moved right, agricultural legislation (particularly the farm bill) is becoming highly contentious (Sheingate 2013). In 2008 Congress easily overrode a presidential veto on the Food, Conservation, and Energy Act, with a final tally of 316 to 108 in the House, and 80 to 14 in the Senate (I return to the story of the 2008 farm bill in Chapter 5). But, just six short years later, in 2013 (one year after the expiration of the 2008 farm bill), the farm bill failed in a floor vote in the House of Representatives. What should have been the 2013 farm bill, titled the Federal Agriculture Reform and Risk Management Act of 2013, was not signed into law as the Agriculture Act until January 2014.

Why did the farm bill struggle so badly in the House of Representatives in 2013? The answer lies in increasing partisan polarization, and specifically in the increasing extremism of Republicans. House Majority Leader Eric Cantor (R-VA) wanted stricter rules on food stamps and a toughening of work requirements for those receiving benefits. Frank Lucas (R-OK), then chairman of the Agriculture Committee balked, knowing that such a move would undercut support from Democrats, both in the committee and on the floor. In response, Cantor pushed an amendment by Steve Southerland (R-FL) that would have achieved these ends and resulted in severe cuts to hunger and nutrition programs (Rogers 2013). When the farm bill came to the floor, Republicans largely voted for the amendment, which (as predicted) undercut Democratic support for the bill. Ultimately, sixty-two conservative Republicans (fifty-eight of whom had voted in favor of the amendment) still ended up voting against the farm bill, saying that it did not cut spending enough; most Democrats also voted against because it cut spending too much. The eventual legislation that landed on President Obama's desk largely resembled the Senate version of the bill, though neither side was pleased with the content. The final version of the bill included $8 billion in cuts to hunger and nutrition programs (largely the Supplemental Nutrition Assistance Program), a far cry from the $40 billion cut that conservative House Republicans had called for but enough to greatly displease most Democrats. And, while lawmakers claimed that it was a bipartisan effort, not a single Republican lawmaker attended the signing of the law, though many were invited (Good 2014).

This struggle hints at a fracturing of the coalition between conservative farm policy advocates and liberal hunger policy advocates—embodied by the famous partnership between Senators Robert Dole and George McGovern—who had previously, consistently worked together on agricultural legislation. If the agricultural subsystem was not open before, it certainly is becoming so now. The current agriculture subsystem is showing telltale signs of being in a moment of instability, a la *Agendas and Instability* (Baumgartner and Jones 1993a; Sheingate 2021). These moments of instability can lead to major policy change, shifting balances of power, or the formation of new coalitions. While it is difficult to tell if the subsystem is on the brink of collapse and reformation, we can tell that rising partisanship is shaking the internal relationships within Congress, and that such instability is extending to the agricultural interests of those who lobby.

And while decoupling efforts have so far failed (or, in the Gingrich case, have been deflected), conservatives have succeeded in reducing funding to food programs (at least, prior to the pandemic), adding additional work requirements, and generally restricting eligibility (Stein 2018). The polarization of previously cross-cutting and generally consensus-building policy areas raises a series of puzzling questions, not just for the study of Congress but also for the study of interest groups. If cross-cutting coalitions within the House Agriculture Committee and the Senate Committee on Agriculture, Nutrition, and Forestry are devolving, is a similar devolution happening within agricultural interest groups? How are interest groups reacting to subsystem instability? What does an increasingly partisan environment do to political advocacy? How does it change interest group strategy, importance, and influence?

PICKING PRODUCE, NOT SIDES

Generally speaking, many ag-sector interest groups are not interested in picking a political "side" ' even though they may become pigeonholed that way. In interviews, a common refrain among lobbyists was that they sought relationships from both Republicans and Democrats and preferred not to be dragged into overtly partisan conflict:

> We have to continue to try to find our opportunities for finding that bi-partisan support because . . . if you just get one side loving you, at some point the other side is going to be in charge and then you're left out in the dark for eight years.[6]

Most interest groups are looking for a particularized outcome that benefits their members; corporations, in particular, seek outcomes that benefit their bottom lines. Their preferences may situate them in closer alignment with one party or another, but ultimately, they'll take any and all support they can find, from either side of the aisle. Many lobbyist groups speak, at least perfunctorily, even to legislators who they know oppose their agenda. Interviewed lobbyists often emphasized the point that, while they strive to keep communication lines open, they are still outsiders trying to influence the process; they don't presume to know what will happen or how any individual legislator will ultimately behave. As Chuck Conner of the National Council of Farmer Cooperatives, put it:

> This is crazy business. You never know for sure where people are going to come from. I could cite you numerous examples where [you think], "Wow, I can't believe he did that." So you never totally give up on any-body. It's part of good transparency, good courtesy.[7]

Keeping legislators apprised of their agenda respectfully, across party aisles, maintains relationships, opens lines of communication, and builds interest group reputation. The way that interest groups go about this process, whether through grassroots advocacy or personal contacts, often depends on how much support the group has in the member's home district (Hojnacki and Kimball 1998). Even so, building strong relationships with as many offices as possible remains important for interest groups seeking influence. Relationships and reputations are the currency of advocacy (LaPira and Thomas 2017). As Ferd Hoefner, of the generally "progressive" National Sustainable Agriculture Coalition, observed:

> *Trust goes a long way in this business. They may completely disagree with you, but they may trust that your information is accurate. They might disagree with us but they understand that we have thousands of farmer members who actually feel this way.*[8]

But relationships, like Rome, are not built in a day; given this, wealthier interest groups find themselves with a considerable advantage in the lobbying game. This is true both in terms of horizontal (lobbyist to lobbyist) and vertical (lobbyist to legislator) relationships. While public attention is often focused on those vertical, lobbyist–legislator relationships, lobbyists know that their horizontal relationships can be just as important and can facilitate more productive vertical relationships. Research on coalition building shows that for policy advocates, constructing an "interest-diverse" coalition can be invaluable in gaining legislative and regulatory traction (Dwidar 2021; Lorenz 2019; Nelson and Yackee 2012).

When it comes to vertical relationships, relationships with committee members and more senior legislators are particularly essential to the business of advocacy, as these are the members of Congress who are most able to influence the contents of legislation through the provision of information to fellow members (Grier and Munger 1993; Stratmann 1991). In this regard, the advantage goes to those interest groups that can afford to hire "revolving-door" lobbyists, who have a legislative background and existing relationships on Capitol Hill, and groups that can afford to maintain and sustain their lobbying presence over the long term (Lux, Crook, and Woehr 2011; Mathur and Singh 2011).

GRIDLOCK AND GROUNDHOG DAY

This dual advantage for wealthier groups able to hire more connected lobbyists and sustain lobbying efforts for longer periods of times has grown larger as political polarization has set in. And polarization in Congress is at a historical high point; as Voteview data in Figure 3.1 show. The ideological distance between the parties, in both the House and the Senate, is wider than ever before, quite literally.

Partisan polarization has two significant impacts on the legislative process: increased competition for agenda setting, and increased gridlock at particularly contentions points in the process. Not only is it harder to get an item on the agenda of action, it also gets harder to resolve any disputes. In this regard, polarization in Congress also leads to heightened attention on any piece of legislation (e.g., the farm bill in 2013) as partisan bickering breaks out over even the most minor points, which in turn gets interest groups more involved (Baumgartner and Jones 1993a; Baumgartner and Leech 2001; Schattschneider 1957). Interest groups "bandwagon" as

Figure 3.1 Liberal–conservative partisan polarization by chamber (Lewis et al. 2021)

attention increases, and flock to whichever venue other interest groups are lobbying in (Baumgartner and Leech 2001). In short, partisan polarization increases interest group competition in the subsystem, and more interest group attention to an issue functionally broadens conflict and increases inter-group competition (Schattschneider 1957), although in some instances it also offers more opportunity for coalition-building (more on this later).

Simultaneously to increasing conflict and attention—and because of it—partisanship also leads to increased gridlock, which slows down the policy process. Binder shows that "despite the faith of responsible party advocates in *cohesive* political parties . . . policy change is *less* likely as the parties become more polarized and the percentage of moderate legislators shrinks" (1999, 527). Stronger party unity may make it easier for Democrats or Republicans to achieve policy victories during times when they overwhelmingly control both chambers and the presidency but, as Binder shows, conditions of increased partisan polarization slow down legislating and result in more gridlock, overall. An example of this, given by a legislative staffer, illustrates the challenge of the shrinking middle in political parties.

> *I think in all areas it's definitely become more partisan. That's plainly obvious. But I think in farm policy we're in a unique spot where, you know we've lost all of our rural Democrats; the Blue Dogs are gone. They used to be kind of a part of the coalition. There's only a handful of those left. . . . Yet we have Republican members, a significant number of Republican members in the House, that consistently vote against farm policy because they brought on this limited-government kind of platform. We saw it with Tim Huelskamp in Kansas, where finally they were able to overthrow him, but it took several tries. You would think that someone that votes against the farm bill [would get kicked out]. [How someone] who's just so anti agriculture could represent a district that produces [so much]. . . . And so there is really that disconnect. . . . You talk about lower taxes you talk about limited government. That's great. But this thing that's one quarter of one percent of the entire*

federal budget is a huge deal to people back home. So focus your attention on it, on the issues that . . . really do drive the debt and [don't] spend so much time obsessing over this little small sliver. The challenge is ideological congruency and the need to meet the actual needs of your home district constituents and communicating that.[9]

Increased conditions of gridlock do not imply that legislating has completely stopped or has truly ground to a halt. Obviously, Congress still legislates and regulates. In fact, at times, Congress does very big and important things (think: Obamacare, financial sector reform, and the regular passage of omnibus bills). Now the legislative process follows a sustained pattern of punctuated equilibrium (Baumgartner and Jones 1993b). That is, as Congress becomes more partisan, the policy process has become longer—the periods of stasis (also known as gridlock) are more prolonged, and alterations to the status quo are less frequent though possibly larger (Brock and Mallinson, forthcoming)—a change to which lobbyists are highly attuned. In one interview, a lobbyist explained his experience with the increasingly challenging environment on the Hill: "I think it's becoming increasingly important because it's increasingly difficult to get meaningful legislation through Congress because there are so many opportunities to move members on these issues and messages can get distorted so quickly."[10]

Policy changes that used to be a "sure thing" are now in doubt and must be pursued doggedly to passage. He further explained, "I find the issues that should have been a lighter lift become a Herculean lift."[11] Another lobbyist described it as feeling reminiscent of Groundhog Day: "You're going back and talking about the same issue [year after year],"[12] while another described being "stuck in a situation where nothing moves rapidly, if at all."[13]

Polarization-fueled gridlock means that lobbyists must work harder, and longer, to persevere through a slower process. Simultaneously, increased attention to issues, driven by partisanship, means that interest groups face more competition for attention and influence. *Lobbying with any impact requires effort sustained over a longer period of time to see success, and the effort required is growing as more groups compete for attention.* Therefore, lobbying is becoming more expensive in the sheer length of time and long-term maintenance required from interest groups seeking to advocate on an issue. Such conditions naturally elevate the privilege of groups able to afford a sustained, long-term advocacy strategy in Washington, DC, both because those groups will be able to continuously cultivate their relationships (with other aligned lobbying groups and with legislators) and because they have the financial capacity to sustain lobbying efforts over multiple sessions.

COMMUNICATION SUBSIDIES

Groups able to play the long game do so by providing services, or "subsidies," to members eager to obtain help. One such subsidy is communication. This subsidy is critical because another common side effect of polarization is less communication between members of Congress. In far less polarized times, members from both parties socialized more frequently; some even shared Capitol Hill apartments to cut down on living expenses while their families stayed back in the home districts. Examples of such relationships from the 1970s and 1980s abound. Democratic Speaker of the House Tip O'Neill (D-MA), a man who was *highly partisan* on the House floor, famously had close personal friendships with politicians from across the aisle, including President Ronald Reagan. In one notable exchange, Tip O'Neill appeared on a talk show saying that Regan had "no concern, no regard, no care for the little man of America," to which Reagan responded that O'Neill used "sheer demagoguery" in politics; the next day on the phone, when Reagan called to apologize, O'Neill told him, "Old buddy, that's politics—after 6 o'clock we can be friends, but before 6 it's politics" (Burns 2012). O'Neill was also close to Republican House member Silvio Conte (R-MA), who once said of O'Neill, "Few people have a greater impact on my life than my mentor, my friend and my conscience across the aisle" (Burns 2012). Today, however, such bipartisan socializing is rare, replaced by acrimonious relationships with members across the aisle. Consider House Representative Marjorie Taylor Greene (R-GA) announcing at her victory party, "We're going to kick that bitch [Nancy Pelosi] out of Congress," after which she received a congratulatory phone call from House Minority Leader Kevin McCarthy (Draper 2022). A short time later, Greene chased her Democratic colleague, House Representative Alexandria Ocasio-Cortez (D-NY), down a hallway full of reporters while yelling, "Alexandria! Alexandria! Why won't you debate me?" (Draper 2022). From watching the behavior of certain members, one might think that collegial communication is dead, or at least, it is certainly unwell and perhaps increasingly rare. This decline of collegiality fundamentally changes the way that members interact with each other, as well as the role that lobbyists play in the proverbial iron triangle (the informal but tight-knit decision-making structure that is said to exist between interest groups, bureaucrats, and congressional committees).

One lobbyist emphasized that it is essential to communicate with every member of Congress, not just to keep communication lines open but also because members of Congress may not be speaking with each other regularly, or cordially. As one lobbyist explained:

> *You shouldn't assume that the offices are talking to each other. . . . You need to make sure that you know your messages are being communicated. You need to go out there and talk to each office individually, so they share information.*[14]

Compounding the slower and more punctuated process of legislating and the partisan breakdown of communication is the changing power structure of Congress, and, in particular, an increased reliance on committee leadership, related to the decreased time rank-and-file members are allowed to read and analyze legislation (Curry 2015). Today's legislators have a reduced institutional capacity on which to rely. They spend more time on campaigning and constituency services, they no longer have bipartisan committee staff, and there are generally fewer committee resources.

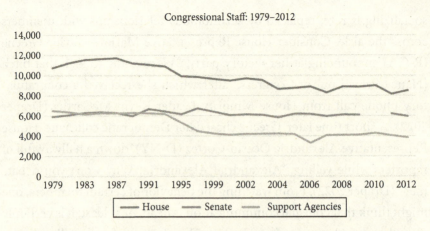

Figure 3.2 Decline in congressional staff and support agencies between 1979 and 2009. Data are from The Brookings Institution's *Vital Statistics on Congress* (see Reynolds 2021). Data for Senate staff are unavailable for the year 2010.

The decline in institutional capacity, in particular, is related to the steady decrease in employment of congressional staff and support. Figure 3.2 illustrates a slow but steady decline in the employment of both congressional staffers who might offer in-office research support, as well as a decline in employment at the congressional support agencies who have traditionally offered nonpartisan support and analysis. These support agencies, specifically, include the General Accountability Office, the Congressional Research Service, the Congressional Budget Office, and, prior to 1995, the Office of Technology Assessment. Notably, the Office of Technology Assessment was eliminated in 1995 by the new House GOP majority led by Newt Gingrich, which saw its work as inefficient and largely as rationalizing government regulation (Sadowski 2012).

In many ways, Congress has ceded its analytic capacity to outside interests (LaPira and Thomas 2017, 77). Such outsourcing means that there are fewer congressionally employed minds or eyes on the issues, giving further credence to the adage, "Attention in Washington is scarce" (Baumgartner et al. 2009, 22).

In conjunction with fewer resources and staff support, there is a slow restriction of information and communication available to rank-and-file members in particular. Leadership increasingly keeps information from rank-and-file members as a tool to force compliance and party unity (Curry 2015, 78). Members not only have greater fundraising and campaigning demands on their time, they also have less access to reliable information from leadership or their fellow legislators about legislation. Interest groups expressing support or opposition to legislation, then, act as important signals regarding the potential political or electoral consequences of supporting a particular bill (Curry 2015, 67; Hansen 1991). The role of interest groups as adjunct congressional staff has been long established (Bauer, Pool, and Dexter 1963), but the centrality of that role is steadily increasing because of changing conditions in Congress.

COALITIONAL SUBSIDIES

Not only are groups increasingly responsible for providing critical information, they also seem more responsible for building the very coalitions needed to pass legislation. Increased polarization, the lack of communication among members, and the hoarding of information by party leaders all mean that interest groups and their lobbyists must work harder and longer than ever to overcome congressional gridlock (some might call it institutional friction). In interviews, lobbyists described working over longer time horizons to see legislation through to passage due to a generally slower legislative process. This means spending more money. Some groups will be able to engage in this level of sustained lobbying independently; many will not. This leads to the question, how can interest groups continue to lobby vocally and successfully as the legislative process becomes even slower and more opaque? Additionally, given the scarcity of attention in Washington, how do lobbyists overcome the noise and stand out? My interviews suggest that the best strategy for this is to specialize in coalition-building.

Political scientists have argued that "government has essentially outsourced its brainpower to the lobbying community" (LaPira and Thomas 2017, 51). My interviews suggest that interest groups that can provide not only information but also the cover and credibility of a coalition create a relatively lower risk opportunity for members of Congress to support their issues. Interest groups now go beyond providing information (aka brain power). These interviews suggest that, with increasing frequency, coalition-building is occurring externally to Congress rather than within it. Interest groups can, if they are skilled and resourced enough, create a *coalitional subsidy* for members by doing the work of finding, building, and negotiating coalitions around policy. Legislators know information is valuable if it has a ready-made coalition of external support behind it. This also lowers the cost of supporting legislation. Interest groups can essentially become nonpartisan negotiators, and, in doing so, can provide cover to members of Congress and make it easier for them to support legislation (or oppose it). Additionally, failing to advocate in a bipartisan way can undermine the efficacy of advocacy groups, even when lawmakers recognize that the substance of their message is credible. A legislative staffer gave an example of an interest group that was trying to counter a report from the Heritage Foundation, a well-known right-wing think tank:

> *You know in hindsight the organizations that, that organized those papers and sponsored those rebuttals probably would have been better served if [they had fought] back against a right-wing think tank, [if they had] someone that has Republican bona fides to be able to make that response even if the arguments were identical. It's just the sauce, you know.*[15]

The "sauce" in this case was a critical component in the difficulty that an interest group faced in successfully pushing back against ideas that were, according to this staffer, poorly formulated. This staffer also made a point that many interest groups recognized but not all could afford to accommodate. Staff and offices listen more closely to lobbyists who have a partisan background similar to their own. Advocacy groups and companies who are relatively more well-funded can afford to hire multiple lobbyists, and some advocacy groups discussed strategically sending revolvers[16] with appropriate political backgrounds to talk with legislators of the same partisanship. But many other groups do not have the finances or bandwidth to hire different lobbyists to target different legislators. A group that cannot hire multiple lobbyists should, at a minimum, think carefully about the way it frames its message, or its "pitch method" as one lobbyist termed it, to provide political cover and commonality to members who may need additional reasons to support an idea or initiative.

The full consequences of all of this for policymaking are not yet clear. It has always been difficult to disentangle exactly how much influence lobbyists have over legislative outcomes. But the evidence presented here suggests that because lobbying is more time-consuming and requires more investment of resources (coalition building is *hard*, and it can be expensive), it is likely going to be even harder for small or under-resourced groups to have a voice. Additionally, only well-resourced groups are likely to have the finances to hire both Republican and Democratic lobbyists, since revolving-door lobbyists are significantly more costly to hire than those who have non-political backgrounds (LaPira and Thomas 2017). Together these features of the political environment suggest that the lobbying landscape will likely become even more lopsided in favor of groups with deep pockets and big resources. However, coalition-building can help groups with shallower pockets have a voice if they can organize.

Polarization is transforming the nature and impact of lobbying. As the political ground shifts, lobbying groups are forced to change their strategies for influence. An increasingly polarized and gridlocked policymaking environment means that interest groups must be prepared to lobby in a more sustained and collaborative manner in order to influence policy outcomes. This is because influence comes in two forms: informational and coalitional subsidies for elected officials who increasingly spend their time at home campaigning with constituents rather than legislating on the Hill; and coalitional subsidies, through which lobbyists can provide the kinds of connections and political cover that members need to accomplish legislative change or protect the status quo. Established and well-financed groups and corporations are naturally better equipped to sustain lobbying efforts through gridlocked political battles that rage over multiple sessions and are therefore able to exert more influence. However, other groups may overcome their resource-disadvantages if they are skilled at forming coalitions with other interest groups, especially unlikely allies. The hurdle is high, but so are the potential rewards.

4

The (Not Quite) Business as Usual of Washington

Corporate Lobbying Strategies

Many years ago, there was a senator from Alabama, by the name of Howell Heflin, who served on the Ag committee throughout his tenure. He saw a lot of farm bills come and go, and for three consecutive farm bills, when we would meet in the Senate, the first day of debate he would give his opening speech. He would always say, "Mr. Chairman, I don't know why we're here meeting yet, because we can't talk about the farm bill because all the Ag lobbyists haven't decided what they want yet in the farm bill!" And everybody would always laugh, and they knew the speech was coming, but he was right on target. Ultimately, members of Congress, when it comes to Agricultural policy, sort out opinions from their various friends in the Ag community, from organizations like ours. They're seeking the groups' input.[1]

—CHUCK CONNER, *National Council of Farmer Cooperatives,*

Washington, DC, August 2014

Interest groups, businesses, associations—and the lobbyists they hire—rely on a wide variety of lobbying tactics and techniques. Their aims are

Farmed Out. Clare R. Brock, Oxford University Press. © Clare R. Brock 2024.
DOI: 10.1093/oso/9780197683798.003.0004

informative and persuasive, and their audiences often receptive. Lobbyists play an integral role in the creation of public policy by informing lawmakers of stakeholders' preferences as well as apprising them of political considerations, most notably, any potential reelection consequences (Hansen 1991). When the Healthy, Hunger-Free Kids Act was passed in 2010, neither lawmakers nor interest groups fully anticipated the conflicts that would arise as details were hammered out during regulation. But corporations, especially frozen food manufacturers that supply meals to schools, quickly learned just how impactful the legislation stood to be, especially to their bottom lines.

Around the same time, as the Agricultural Act of 2014 began to take shape, interest groups swarmed to get some piece of the pie. In fact, that year the farm bill was the sixth most heavily lobbied measure on Capitol Hill (Feinberg 2014). Leading the charge, alongside a variety of notable agricultural interest groups, was Monsanto (now a division of Bayer). The chemical company, a giant among crop and seed producers, spent $36 million on lobbying activities in the five years preceding passage of the bill. And, while final legislation included billions of dollars in cuts to food stamps and conservation programs, it also included a $7 billion increase to crop insurance, to be doled out over the next decade (Feinberg 2014). Increases in federal support for crop insurance may be advertised as helping farmers, but these increases also help companies that provide those farmers with basic supplies, hence Monsanto's keen interest.

Of course, to say that lobbying alone resulted in these outcomes would be misleading at best, and patently false at worst. Republicans, who then controlled the House, had been seeking to cut spending on SNAP and actively worked toward those ends; at the same time, the Republicans on the House Agriculture Committee tend to represent agricultural districts. In short, the fights surrounding the farm bill, and its eventual contents, represent some combination of the consequences of partisan motivation, constituency representation, and interest group advocacy. After all, even Monsanto is a constituent, in a fashion.

This chapter[2] uses business, or firm, lobbying in the agricultural subsystem to assess how lobbying behavior has changed between 1998 and

2013. Firms are certainly not the only types of groups that lobby. Public interest groups, trade associations, and even state governments also engage in lobbying. However, businesses dominate the lobbying landscape across every industry. In lobbying, broadly, businesses have spent between $22 and $35 on lobbying for every $1 spent by diffuse interest groups and unions combined (Drutman 2015, 13). Agriculture holds out as a relatively less corporate sector, and yet, nearly 25 percent of lobbying done in the livestock sector can be attributed to companies; around 30 percent of crop production and basic processing lobbying is done by companies; and almost 100 percent of tobacco lobbying can be accounted for by looking at corporate lobbying (Drutman 2015, 111). Corporate lobbying is by no means the only type of lobbying, but it is significant and worth study on its own merit.

Firm-level analysis is particularly useful because the additional available data on firms, such as headquarters location and revenue, allow for the possibility that resources and political connections further complicate the impact of partisan polarization on behavior. This chapter explores how firm lobbying behavior has changed over time—they may be increasing their lobbying toward some institutions but not others—and who is advantaged and disadvantaged in this new political context. The evidence regarding these changes illustrates that political polarization has significant implications for whose voice is heard on Capitol Hill.

CORPORATE LOBBYISTS: BRAINPOWER AND INFLUENCE

Lobbying has increased steadily in recent decades (Drutman 2015). It is well established that one of the primary roles of lobbyists is to provide informational subsidies to members of Congress (Baumgartner et al. 2009; Baumgartner and Leech 1998; de Figueiredo 2002; Hansen 1991). A legislative, or informational, subsidy from a lobbyist is "a matching grant of policy information, political intelligence, and legislative labor to the enterprises of strategically selected legislators . . . to assist natural allies in achieving their own, coincident objectives" (Hall and Deardorff 2006, 69).

There are several explanations as to why this behavior is increasing, and regarding what kind of information lobbyists are providing to legislators. One answer as to why lobbying is increasing over time is that it is a self-perpetuating industry. Legislators welcome the informational subsidies provided by lobbyists, and lobbyists are incentivized to create demand for their services (Drutman 2015). Another explanation is conflict expansion: government expands to legislate a greater variety of issues, and, in the expansion, greater numbers of industries and businesses are affected by regulation. As this occurs, the discussion over who and what the new laws will impact, and how these laws will be operationalized, creates a potentially endless expansion of conflict space (Baumgartner and Jones 1993; Schattschneider 1960). Further, as the scope of conflict expands, so do the variety, depth, and complexity of the information that Congress needs in order to do its job, even as members spend increasingly large amounts of time on campaign activities and constituency services. Faced with an opportunity to fill in information gaps, lobbyists increase their activity in response to congressional demand for the information that they are so adept at providing (LaPira and Thomas 2017; Leech et al. 2005). Finally, lobbying may be expanding simply because it is profitable, particularly for corporations (Alexander, Mazza, and Scholz 2009; Drutman 2015; Waterhouse 2015). Lobbyists are sensitive to "policy windows" such as moments of major regulatory reforms (Alexander, Mazza, and Scholz 2009) and budgeting discussions (de Figueiredo 2004), and they are cognizant of the potential profitability of lobbying during these times. These explanations are not necessarily mutually exclusive; they describe the moving parts of the current political climate, and they work together to generate business for the advocacy industry.

This book adds an additional component to that: partisan polarization. Beginning in the 1990s, House and Senate Republicans became increasingly ideologically cohesive and partisan, and began voting much more coherently as a party bloc rather than as individual members with unique interests (Theriault 2013). The intensification of partisanship, particularly among the "Gingrich senators," has resulted in a marked decline in collegiality and a corresponding uptick in hostility (Theriault 2013). In short, Congress has experienced a rise in "combative conservatism" (Grossmann and Hopkins 2016, 285).

In tandem with the increase of partisan hostility, Congress suffered a decline in its institutional capacity for gathering and assessing information (Curry 2015; Drutman 2015; LaPira and Thomas 2017). This decline occurred for two main reasons. First, congressional leadership began restricting information to rank-and-file members (Curry 2015); and second, members spend increasingly more time on campaign activities and constituency services (LaPira and Thomas 2017). Over time, congressional leadership has used information restriction as a key exercise of power and party control over other members; this strategy ensures that legislators, often lacking the time and resources to study the legislation themselves and preoccupied with the perpetual demands of fundraising, are forced to turn to their party leaders for information and guidance (Curry 2015). Additionally, Congress eroded its own capacity for information gathering and analysis over the years, arguably starting with the elimination of the Office of Technology Assessment (OTA) in 1995, by reducing employment of nonpartisan committee staff and allocating resources away from research in favor of performing more constituency services and seeking reelection (LaPira and Thomas 2017). The loss of experienced high-ranking, senior committee staff has been particularly detrimental to congressional committee effectiveness and productivity (Ommundsen 2022). Congressional staffers—overworked, underpaid, and often inexperienced—are often forced to play "intellectual catch-up" on more technical matters of policymaking, and frequently turn to lobbyists to explain highly complex or technical policy for them. Such dependence gives lobbyists enormous power over policy details and content (Drutman 2015, 233). In short, lobbyists function as adjunct staffers (Boehmke, Gailmard, and Patty 2013; Hall and Deardorff 2006; LaPira and Thomas 2017) and provide information in response to congressional demand for that information (Leech et al. 2005). As LaPira and Thomas observe, "the government has essentially outsourced its brainpower to the lobbying community" (2017, 51).

Corporate America is one of the primary communities providing that brainpower. Business and corporate interests are disproportionately over-represented among groups lobbying Congress (Baumgartner and Leech 1998; Boehmke, Gailmard, and Patty 2013; Drutman 2015; de Figueiredo 2004). Take the example from Chapter 1 of the powerful influence exerted by a single frozen foods company in shaping school lunch regulations. While policy images within the agricultural-oriented areas of the food policy subsystem still evoke small-town family farmers, the reality is dominance by companies and trade associations. Tobacco, for instance, consistently rates among one of the highest spending industries, and nearly 100 percent of that spending is done by companies in the industry (Drutman 2015, 111). Lobbying in the sector of "crop production" represents a more diverse playing field, in the sense that both farmers and companies are politically active. Yet still around 40 percent of all lobbying done in this sector is done by companies (Drutman 2015, 111), and the farmers themselves are not necessarily those folksy family farmers, given that over 66 percent of US farm goods are produced from just a few large-scale production farms (Klein and Locke 2014).

THE DIRT ON POLARIZATION AND LOBBYING

If lobbyists provide necessary policy and electoral information to members of Congress, then how does party polarization change that relationship, if at all? Polarization has certainly changed which issues attract the most attention—partisan issues are often more salient, and receive more news coverage, than nonpartisan issues (Baumgartner et al. 2009). But does polarization change how lobbyists themselves behave?

Agribusiness interests are lobbying in an environment in which rank-and-file members of Congress have both less time and less information. Further, as members spend less time on the Hill, they enjoy fewer relationships and less collegiality among themselves, a condition exacerbated by party polarization (Theriault 2013). Lobbyists are providing information that members of Congress once communicated among themselves, including pivotal vote counts. "Lobbyists fill the vacuum created by partisanship," Andres (2009) notes. "Polarization has strengthened their hand in a process where information—particularly intelligence about what is happening on the other side of the aisle—is a highly valuable commodity" (116). This role aligns with the established wisdom that skilled agricultural and agribusiness lobbyists are providing not only policy expertise but also valuable political information (Hansen 1991). In short, lobbyists no longer provide just an information subsidy, they also provide a *communication subsidy*—establishing key communications to and between members of Congress, including legislative strategy information such as vote counts and other insider details that members once communicated directly to each other or that would have been communicated by committee leadership. Indeed, members of Congress count on this. Evidence suggests that as partisan hostility has increased, conservative members, in particular, have developed a strategy of cultivating corporations and encouraging them to hire Republican lobbyists in order to bolster their influence on legislation (Grossmann and Hopkins 2016, 292). In other words, members of Congress make a deliberate choice to rely on lobbyists, particularly those who share their ideological preferences and corporate interests. The increased hostility among members of Congress, decreased flows of information, and greater political reliance on lobbyists have expanded the opportunities for business groups, in particular, to have powerful influence in the construction of public policy. In sum, party polarization has increased the already substantial influence of business over legislation (evoking McConnell 1966 and Andres 2009, among others).

The idea that polarization has increased the political demand for the informational and communicative subsidies is not a novel or surprising idea to lobbyists in the agricultural sector; indeed, it is a new reality about which they are abundantly aware. In interviews, agriculture and food sector lobbyists suggested that they have changed how they approach Congress, and Washington more broadly, since the era of party polarization began. An agribusiness trade association lobbyist baldly explained, "[Polarization] is making things harder. And I think it's making people work harder and making them have to spend more time."[3] In practical terms, this suggests that while polarization may give lobbyists increased influence over legislation (Andres 2009), it also forces them to work harder and longer for desirable political outcomes (more on this in Chapters 5 and 6). Research regarding lobbying in state governments has also indicated that conflict and hostility between parties gives lobbyists more power over legislation, but simultaneously that advocacy groups must dedicate more resources and work harder to be successful in influencing state legislators (Bullock and Padgett 2007). Given this, we should expect that interest groups will lobby Congress (the bastion of partisan tension), but not the White House or bureaucracy, at a higher volume during times of partisan polarization. To show that it is partisan polarization driving changes to lobbying, rather than some broad increase in lobbying, this chapter uses that comparison across institutions to test the hypothesis that *partisan polarization in Congress increases the amount of lobbying directed at Congress, but not the amount of lobbying directed at the White House or agencies.*

This is not an argument about venue shopping, in which lobbyists are looking for a receptive institutional audience and shift their focus accordingly, although this certainly occurs (Holyoke 2016). Rather, I am using lobbying of the White House and bureaucracy as comparison points for advocacy behavior. Consistent with existing findings in the literature, I expect that lobbying in Congress will be closely related with lobbying in other venues (Boehmke, Gailmard, and Patty 2013). However, in the agricultural sector in particular, the congressional environment has changed—it is increasingly characterized by bitter partisanship and the accompanying "gridlock" so frequently associated with these fights—with consequent impacts on lobbying in Congress.

Given the constant lament about gridlock in Congress, we should perhaps not be surprised that lobbyists must work harder now than ever before, though that hard work is possibly rewarded by greater influence. However, political science has yet to clearly show the link between partisan polarization and increased lobbying. In the following sections I test whether this phenomenon is simply one of perception among bedraggled lobbyists, or if it is the new political reality facing policy advocates.

TRENDS IN LOBBYING BEHAVIOR

To test the theories put forward, this book relies on both interviews and an original dataset of lobbying reports to explain how lobbyists are responding to polarization in the food and agriculture policy arena. All statistical analysis contained in this book begins with the year 1998 and extends through the year 2013. This time frame begins when lobbying disclosure act data first become available and extends through the construction of the 2014 farm bill.

Although the Agricultural Act of 2014 was passed and signed into law on February 7, 2014, most of the action for the legislation, up to and including the meeting of the conference committee, occurred in 2013. In October 2013, the House and Senate versions of what would become the farm bill were still quite far apart. From October through mid-December, the conference committee worked hard to reconcile the two versions of the bills, with surprising bipartisanship among committee members (which largely did not reflect the positions of their colleagues in the rank and file) (Bosso 2017). However, Congress adjourned for its winter break before it was able to vote on the conference committee report and pass the legislation into law. In January the conference committee continued to work out the remaining details and compromises, and the ultimate result "offered everyone something to dislike" (Bosso 2017, 149). Ultimately, the law represented relatively modest changes from previous farm bills, and yet, in spite of bipartisan construction and passage, no Republicans were present as President Obama signed the bill into law. Though the dataset for this book ends just before the signing of the bill, interviews were conducted in 2014, just after its passage, and again in 2018, months before the passage of the Agriculture Improvement Act of 2018.

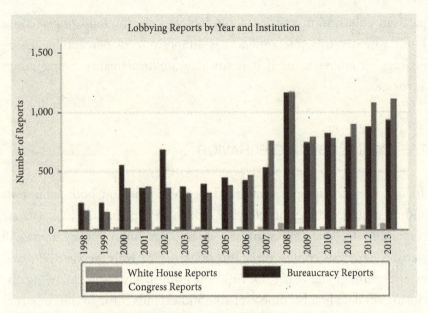

Figure 4.1 Total agriculture lobbying reports by institution and year

Interviews are particularly useful to understand the *why* behind the data analysis presented here. One reason is that lobbying disclosure act (LDA) data are limited in their scope and often are challenging to parse effectively. For detail about the dataset, the pitfalls, challenges, and benefits of LDA data, and justifications of the methods used, see Appendix A. For this chapter, I use LDA data, paired with firm-level data. The dependent variable in the analysis that follows, and throughout much of the book, is described as "reports" of lobbying, by institution.

Between 1998 and 2013 lobbying increased steadily, across all institutions. Figure 4.1 illustrates the number of reports made by firms during that time span, by institution. It is important to note that the number of reports filed (the dependent variable) nearly doubles in 2008, after new reporting requirements went into effect (this is controlled for in the analysis that follows).

Simultaneously, while the volume of lobbying done by individual firms was steadily increasing, so was the number of firms engaged in lobbying in the agricultural space (see Figure 4.2). There are noticeable spikes in the

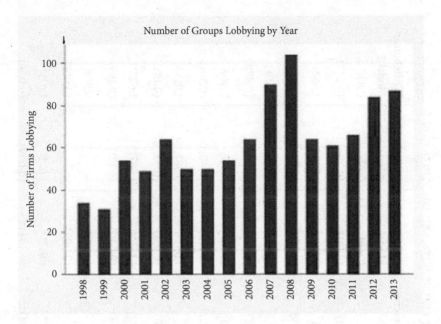

Figure 4.2 Number of firms lobbying on agricultural issues, by year

number of firms engaging in advocacy during those years when Congress was considering a farm bill.

In order to test the hypothesis that polarization increases the quantity of lobbying directed toward Congress, I performed a negative binomial regression on the cross-sectional, time-series data described in Table 4.1. The dependent variable for each regression, respectively, is the number of lobbyists a firm reported hiring to lobby Congress, the bureaucracy, or the White House, in a given year.

One important characteristic of lobbying behavior, indicated by the over-dispersion of the data, is that most groups lobby somewhat inconsistently, and often lobby relatively little when they do report lobbying (meaning that the data are skewed). Figure 4.3 illustrates this skewedness by showing histograms of the number of firms that file just one or two reports over the sixteen years, and the very small number of firms that file many more reports during that same time period. Among the universe of firms that reported lobbying, the mean number of lobbying reports that a firm filed for lobbying Congress in a given year was 10, with the minimum

Table 4.1 LOBBYING BEHAVIOR DIRECTED AT CONGRESS, BUREAUCRACIES, AND THE WHITE HOUSE

	Congress	Congress Model 2	Bureaucracy	Bureaucracy Model 2	Whitehouse	Whitehouse Model 2
Farm Bill Year	0.827	0.832	0.926	0.930	0.826	0.830
	(0.107)	(0.108)	(0.141)	(0.141)	(0.296)	(0.297)
Average Polarization	10.627*	10.868*	0.305	0.297	1.535	1.564
	(11.213)	(11.482)	(0.379)	(0.370)	(4.223)	(4.306)
Divided Congress	1.007	1.010	1.112	1.114	1.438	1.436
	(0.133)	(0.134)	(0.168)	(0.169)	(0.488)	(0.488)
Unified Government	1.201	1.191	0.940	0.936	0.906	0.906
	(0.148)	(0.147)	(0.130)	(0.129)	(0.301)	(0.301)
Committee Connections	1.002	1.065**	1.011	1.053	0.981	1.016
	(0.008)	(0.024)	(0.010)	(0.031)	(0.027)	(0.135)
Revenue, Normalized	1.131**	1.195**	1.133**	1.177**	1.587**	1.627**
	(0.019)	(0.032)	(0.024)	(0.040)	(0.121)	(0.195)
Connections & Revenue Interact	–	0.992**	–	0.995	–	0.996
		(0.003)		(0.003)		(0.014)
Number of Firms Lobbying	1.017**	1.017**	1.013**	1.013**	1.021*	1.021*
	(0.003)	(0.003)	(0.004)	(0.004)	(0.009)	(0.009)

Number of Agriculture Hearings	0.993	0.993	0.995	0.995	0.985	0.985*
	(0.005)	(0.005)	(0.005)	(0.005)	(0.014)	(0.014)
Congress Lobbying	–	–	1.059**	1.059**	1.009	1.009
			(0.005)	(0.003)	(0.007)	(0.008)
Bureaucracy Lobbying	1.066**	1.066**	–	–	1.055**	1.055**
	(0.002)	(0.002)			(0.006)	(0.006)
Whitehouse Lobbying	0.928**	0.928**	1.102**	1.104**	–	–
	(0.022)	(0.022)	(0.026)	(0.026)		
2007 Lay Change Dummy	0.543**	0.542**	0.857	0.856	0.245**	0.245**
	(0.078)	(0.078)	(0.135)	(0.135)	(0.100)	(0.100)
Constant	0.002**	0.001**	0.040**	0.029**	0.000**	0.000**
	(0.002)	(0.000)	(0.039)	(0.029)	(0.001)	(0.000)
N	4,992	4,992	4,992	4,992	4,992	4,992
Wald Chi-Square	1919.51**	1943.26**	1358.14**	1356.81**	317.35	317.87
Log Likelihood	−5246.290	−5242.514	−4424.292	−4423.279	−749.681	−749.645

NOTE: Standard errors appear in parentheses. $^*p \leq 0.05$; $^{**}p \leq 0.01$

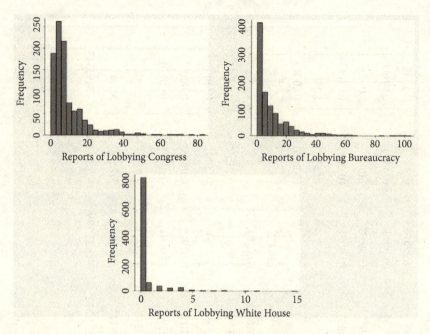

Figure 4.3 Lobbying reports in agriculture by institutional venue

number being 0 and the maximum number being 84. The mean number of reports that a firm filed for lobbying the bureaucracy during the same time period was also 10 and the minimum 0, but the maximum was 104. The White House saw much less lobbying activity, with the mean number of reports at only .5 (most firms reported 0 lobbying in the White House), the minimum being 0, and the maximum being 15 reports. In short, most firms lobby infrequently and often only use one lobbyist or report lobbying on only one issue.

In trying to assess the impact of polarization on lobbying behavior, it is also essential to consider the other environmental and firm characteristics that might also lead to more lobbying over time or in specific cases. Independent variables[4] in the analysis that follows are designed to measure the cyclical nature of decision-making in the agricultural policy space and to capture agenda crowding by accounting for other occasional large pieces of legislation that may attract a sudden influx of advocacy as well as the possibility that some farm bill years are more contentious than others. This is consistent with a theory of congressional demand for lobbying, which indicates that lobbyists are more active at times when Congress is more attentive to their issue areas (Baumgartner et al. 2011; Leech et al. 2005). The independent variables are also intended to capture the known phenomenon of "bandwagoning," when everyone is jumping aboard the lobbying train, so to speak, to avoid being left out (Baumgartner and Leech 1998). I also account for the possibility that lobbyists respond to party control of government (Bullock and Padgett 2007), particularly in a highly polarized partisan environment. Other independent variables account for variation across firms. Only a limited set of firms, generally those with higher revenue, choose to go beyond what can be accomplished through trade associations (Lux, Crook, and Woehr 2011; Mathur and Singh 2011).

Within Congress, lobbyists generally target issue-relevant committees, rather than initiating broad, institution-wide efforts (de Figueiredo and Richter 2013; Hojnacki and Kimball 1998, 1999). Following from this, evidence suggests that when groups enjoy strong constituent ties to a legislator's district they will pursue lobbying, regardless of legislator position (Hojnacki and Kimball 1999). Therefore, I include an independent variable capturing the number of representatives on relevant committees that a firm can claim to be a constituent of, based on the location of a firm's headquarters. I also include a second model with an interaction term between firm revenue and firm location (congressional connections measure). While increased resources provide firms with the capacity to lobby outside of trade associations, on their own behalf, and makes them more likely to do so (Lux, Crook, and Woehr 2011; Mathur and Singh 2011), lobbying organizations (of all kinds) also benefit enormously from the ability to make a constituency-based argument to legislators (de Figueiredo and Richter 2013; Hojnacki and Kimball 1998). The interaction term is intended to capture this phenomenon by accounting for the possibility that firms who are *both* wealthy and particularly well connected may have more influence or power than other firms.

Finally, in each regression, I include the firm reports of lobbying in the other two institutions as independent variables. Lobbying in one institution is a strong predictor of lobbying behavior in another institution because the interest group has already overcome the start-up costs of engaging in advocacy, and because lobbyists are incentivized to create additional markets for themselves (Drutman 2015).

AGRIBUSINESS LOBBYING

The hypothesis suggested that polarization would lead to increased agribusiness lobbying in Congress, as lobbyists responded to a more "gridlocked" environment, but not to increased lobbying in bureaucracies or toward the White House. The results presented in Table 4.1 confirm this hypothesis by showing that polarization has an enormous effect on lobbying behavior directed toward Congress, but not toward the other two institutional venues. The first set of regressions in Table 4.1 is the model without an interaction between firm revenue and committee connections; the second model includes the interaction.

Table 4.1 indicates that party polarization, taken across both chambers, has a large and significant effect on lobbying reports. As predicted by the hypothesis, as polarization increases, agricultural corporation reports of lobbying Congress experience a ten-fold increase. However, reports of lobbying directed toward the bureaucracy and White House do not similarly increase. This suggests that polarization is not increasing lobbying across all venues, but rather that agribusiness firm lobbyists are working harder specifically to achieve preferred outcomes in Congress.

Additionally, regression results across both models show that firm revenue has a considerable and significant impact on lobbying behavior toward all institutions. Firms with higher revenue engage in additional lobbying. This finding is consistent with existing literature on the subject, suggesting that firm resources are a major determinant of corporate lobbying decisions (Drope and Hansen 2006). Predictably, connections to legislators on relevant committees impacted lobbying in Congress, but not in other venues. Similarly, the connections and revenue interaction is significant in Congress only, though with a negative effect. This could perhaps be taken to indicate that firms that enjoy both strong relationships to important members of Congress and high revenue have more political leverage, and therefore enjoy more effective lobbying, facilitating a reduced quantity of advocacy. However, without further investigation such a supposition cannot be proven. This remains an area ripe for future research. In interviews, one plausible explanation for this arose: interest groups who have a strong "grass-roots" base in a district may rely on their employees to do a considerable amount of lobbying in addition to their professional lobbyist—this lobbying, of course, would not be reported under the LDA since regular employees do not spend 51 percent of their time on lobbying activities. One lobbyist reported organizing such lobbying efforts in the following way:

> *I'm more of a facilitator, monitoring what's happening and advocating for my industry. But I also want the people back home, who run the plants and have the jobs, and the lawmakers on capitol hill—I'm a conduit between them, so that the members of Congress have our perspective.*[5]

A member of another group that relies heavily on grassroots lobbying provided another similar explanation, saying, "I don't lobby anybody on Capitol Hill unless we have an economic interest in their district."[6]

Finally, returning to the regression results, the bandwagon effect is clear, as evidenced by the fact that lobbying in any institution is positively associated with lobbying in other venues as well. When an interest group lobbies in one venue, they're likely to lobby elsewhere as well. It is important to note that the regression results offer very little insight into lobbying directed toward the White House, in part because this venue was defined narrowly, and few lobbying reports fell into this category.

FIRM LOBBYING: GROWING LIKE A WEED

Increased firm lobbying toward Congress as a reaction to polarization has two drivers. The first is that, as the lobbyist quoted earlier described, advocacy groups are working much harder and lobbying much more for the same outcomes. The second, which political scientists have worried about (see Andres 2009; Bullock and Padgett 2007), is that polarization and party conflict serve to increase the potential influence of special interests, in turn increasing the incentive to lobby. This is consistent with the logic that lobbying is primarily the *result*, rather than the cause, of governmental activity (Baumgartner et al. 2011), though later I discuss the potential of a positive reinforcement cycle between lobbyist behavior and partisan polarization.

Additionally, the finding that resources and legislative connections are significant predictors of lobbying behavior aligns with what we know from the established literature on the subject (de Figueiredo and Richter 2013; Hojnacki and Kimball 1998). Paired with evidence that party polarization creates additional space for influence, but also requires a greater investment in lobbying, these results suggest that a more polarized political environment is also likely to favor, even more drastically, large and well-resourced corporations. In the agricultural sector such a possibility is particularly notable due to the already lopsided nature of the subsystem. For example, current farm subsidies already reinforce economic disparities between farmers, with the 54 percent of all payments going to just the wealthiest one-tenth of farmers (Reiley 2019). Substantively speaking, an agricultural sector dominated by the largest and most powerful producers and food companies clearly has great influence over American diets, food prices, food access, and conservation policy. Even the anti-hunger sector, which advocates for SNAP and other food and nutrition policies, has a history of partnering with corporate interests to lobby more effectively (Fisher 2017). Indeed, some of the most notorious lobbying groups lobbying on SNAP include the Grocery Manufacturers Association, Coke and Pepsi, Nestlé, Kraft, Walmart, and Kellogg (Fisher 2017, 111). In my interviews, one lobbyist told a story that illustrates the success of that coalition very neatly preventing restrictions on what types of foods could be purchased with SNAP funds:

So, we worked with other food manufacturers, and frankly, advocates in the hunger community who don't like to see these restrictions at all. And together, just lobbied that we think there are better ways to address obesity than to restrict SNAP choices, and that becomes a governmental nightmare trying to decide what's in and what's out. I think what worked most effectively was convincing people that—or just sharing, they didn't really need convincing—but pointing out to people that you might actually end up with bigger government—this worked on the Republican side—rather than smaller, because now you've tasked USDA with coming up with a list of good foods and bad foods. And then, the clerk at the check-out becomes the food police deciding what's in and what's out. It's also—SNAP benefits are supplemental income. These people are typically the working poor, and they have their own money as well. So how do you know whether they're spending their money or SNAP benefits? We worked with the retailers as well, who tell us that it's nearly impossible to program the card with all the three hundred thousand SKUs [stock keeping units] in a grocery store, and keep that up to date, so that it could track what's in and what's out. So very, very complicated. It's a simple concept and very, very hard to put into any practical practice. So, we were successful, there are no restrictions in the farm bill.[7]

As this story illustrates, the potentially increased lobbying power of already wealthy groups relative to the less well-resourced poses a significant concern about the future of American food and agriculture policy, if not democracy more broadly (especially if you are, say, a nutrition advocate who opposes the lack of restrictions on SNAP funding). It also has implications for the types of policy solutions that Congress ultimately considers.

The connection between interest group wealth and lobbying impacts has also been explored elsewhere, with mixed findings. Lobbying *efficacy* is notoriously hard to measure (Baumgartner and Leech 1998). Lobbyists are notoriously unable to sway votes, and often report simply asking members to "just not be too vocally against [legislation]."[8] And yet, it goes against all common sense to believe that lobbying does not have an impact. There is some evidence that corporate lobbying tends to be risk averse and therefore to favor the status quo or to skew toward advocacy toward particularistic benefits that will help their bottom line but do little for the American public, broadly (Drutman 2015). Tests of lobbying efficacy will also fail when the metric is changing floor votes, since roll call voting is notoriously dictated by party affiliation (Poole and Rosenthal 2006). However, more inventive tests of lobbying impact use alternative methods of measuring success such as surveys of lobbyists (McKay 2012) or plagiarism-detection software to trace amendments added to legislation after lobbyist-hosted fundraisers (McKay 2018). These findings support the intuition that there is a link between wealth and policy outcomes. And still in the agricultural sector, corporate lobbying continues to expand, both in quantity and frequency.

Yet another challenge, however, to understanding the relationship between wealth and lobbying is that the number of lobbyists a firm employs does not necessarily indicate their relative quality, connections, or expertise. One proxy for measuring lobbyist efficacy is to look at how much these lobbyists are paid. Lobbyists, for instance, who enjoy more connections to legislators and staffers on Capitol Hill enjoy higher salaries and are more in demand professionally (LaPira and Thomas 2017). However, due to the nature of lobbying disclosure reports, it is impossible to disambiguate lobbying salary while also specifically looking at lobbying activity in a particular policy area. Lobbying disclosure forms report total amount paid to a lobbyist for all advocacy, across all policy areas, and do not allow researchers to see how a lobbyist was paid for their work on a single issue-area. Trying to match lobbyist salary to lobbying activity on a single issue would present challenges, in particular for including contract lobbyists, who may have been paid "less" in a year for their work for a particular company but earned a higher per-hour fee than their in-house counterparts. Further, due to the nature of the LDA data, it is impossible to estimate the amount of money that is being spent by these firms solely on agricultural lobbying, relative to other issue areas, nor do we know specifically which bills industry actors are targeting. In short, LDA data alone do not give us any way to measure the substantive influence of interest groups on legislation; we can only measure the ways and amount in which influence was attempted.

These shortfalls indicate a need for additional revisions to lobbying disclosure requirements. The opacity and limitations of the current system mean that researchers and interested citizens are limited in what they can take from this data. We should therefore be cautious in making dire predictions about the ability of business to determine agricultural legislation, particularly since corporate ability to "buy" legislation is limited and the evidence is mixed (though present—see McKay 2018). Corporations do not lobby unchecked and uncountered, however. The lobbying universe, while lopsided in favor of businesses, still contains multitudes of non-corporate interests. Still, as this book shows, corporate and other well-resourced lobbying partners often enjoy influence not only through independent lobbying but also through coalition-building and partnership with other interests. Chapter 7 returns to the connection between interest group lobbying, interest group wealth, and policy outcomes, and, in particular, explores how corporate wealth impacts firm lobbying decisions and intensity.

5

Keeping Up with the Corporations

Interest Group Adaptation to Party

Polarization in Congress

A historically defining feature of lobbying in agriculture is that interest groups tend to be divided along regional and crop lines, rather than narrowly partisan interests. But over the past two decades, as Congress has become more politically polarized, interest groups have felt the pressure to adapt accordingly. This chapter delves into food and agriculture lobbying behavior across the broad array of lobbying group types, from firms to interest groups, to unions and local governments. In particular, it asks, does polarization increase lobbying across all types of groups, or is this finding exclusive to firms? And does congressional polarization create space for a larger number of groups to lobby, or does it dampen the desire of interest groups to get involved?

As the food and agriculture subsystem finds itself caught in a bitter partisan battle over government spending, particularly on hunger and conservation issues (Good 2014; Neely 2013; Sheingate 2013), regional divisions are being complicated by partisan acrimony. This relatively recent shift in agricultural subsystem dynamics presents the opportunity to look at the behavior changes wrought by sudden polarization. Collectively, we have the opportunity to observe a distinct political shift that changes the lobbying environment for interest groups.

Farmed Out. Clare R. Brock, Oxford University Press. © Clare R. Brock 2024.
DOI: 10.1093/oso/9780197683798.003.0005

It is well established that the United States is in a new era of increased polarization, in which liberals are becoming more liberal, and conservatives more conservative, both in the form of extremism (the median legislator moving away from the center) and in the form of party cohesion (consistency in voting with co-partisans) (Black and Black 2007; Brewer 2005; Poole and Rosenthal 2000; Sinclair 2006; Theriault 2013). The distance between the parties, and between the members therein, is wider now than it has been in recent memory. And this polarization is not only focused on issues that have been historically high salience, like abortion or welfare; its increase is leading to *conflict expansion:* previously noncontroversial issues are becoming newly polarized, and new cleavages are forming where they did not exist before (Layman et al. 2010).

This formation of new cleavages in the agricultural policy space is particularly visible in the passage of farm bills. The House passage of its version of what became the Agricultural Act of 2014, the Agriculture Reform, Food, and Jobs Act of 2013, was possibly one of the most bitterly partisan approval processes in recent farm bill history, as hardline House Republicans worked to separate the Supplemental Nutrition Assistance Program from farm subsidies, or to strip SNAP down to bare bones at the very least (Neely 2013; Sheingate 2013).

It would be easy to claim that the rhetoric around farm bills has always been partisan (and it has), and therefore that such fighting is nothing new. But to illustrate that the protracted 2012–2014 farm bill fight was unique in the way that partisanship fractured historical alliances and displayed remarkable fractures in party-line voting cohesion as a result of partisan extremism, let us return to the story of the 2008 farm bill.

While Gingrich had to be persuaded not to split food stamps into a separate bill in 1996 (and it is notable that he *was* dissuaded from this idea by an Agriculture Committee chair who feared a dissolution of traditional coalitions), the bill nonetheless instituted sweeping changes to farm programs and made significant cuts to SNAP. The next time reauthorization rolled around in 2002, the GOP controlled Congress and George W. Bush reversed many of the freedom-to-farm elements, including restoring SNAP benefits to some individuals who had been excluded under 1996 changes. By 2008, reauthorization in the Democratically controlled House and Senate represented a near total return to "normal" farm bill politics. The 2008 farm bill epitomized "classic Farm Bill politics: offer a bit of something for everyone, from corn ethanol to organic crops; expand nutrition programs; and staple the final package together" (Bosso 2017, 68). The conference version of the bill passed with strong majorities in both the House and Senate; the House vote was 318 to 106 and the Senate vote was 81 to 15 (Food, Conservation, and Energy Act of 2008). Republican President George W. Bush disapproved of the legislation and vetoed the bill on May 21, 2008.[1] President Bush's veto message read:

> For a year and a half, I have consistently asked that the Congress pass a good farm bill that I can sign. Regrettably, the Congress has failed to do so. At a time of high food prices and record farm income, this bill lacks program reform and fiscal discipline. It continues subsidies for the wealthy and increases farm bill spending by more than $20 billion, while using budget gimmicks to hide much of the increase. It is inconsistent with our objectives in international trade negotiations, which include securing greater market access for American farmers and ranchers. It would needlessly expand the size and scope of government. Americans sent us to Washington to achieve results and be good stewards of their hard-earned taxpayer dollars. This bill violates that fundamental commitment. (Bush 2008)

After the president vetoed the legislation, it returned to the House and Senate for a veto override, which passed with the requisite two-thirds support. Unfortunately, after passing the legislation, lawmakers discovered a clerical error which had omitted thirty-five pages of the bill, containing important farm-export and food-aid programs (Abbott 2008). Due to the error, Congress was forced to reintroduce and pass the legislation again, which President Bush then vetoed once again. Congress again overrode the veto; ultimately, the legislation was voted on a total of four times before becoming law. House Majority Leader Steny Hoyer (D-MD) told the press, "This bill is one of the most-passed bills we've done" (Abbott

2008). And importantly, in spite of the Republican president's veto, the 2008 farm bill had sufficient Republican support to pass in Congress (with wide enough margins to overcome a veto) *four times*. Indeed, in the Senate, the opposition was comprised of two Democrats and thirteen Republicans, meaning that thirty-six Republicans voted in favor of the bill—four times. Reuters explained the remarkable bipartisan effort in the following way: "In an election year, a large majority of lawmakers, including many Republicans, backed the farm bill rather than stand with an unpopular president" (Abbott 2008). The *New York Times* made a similar claim, arguing that "the willingness of so many Republicans to break with the White House reflected both the strong support for the bill and a growing alarm among many lawmakers about their election prospects in November" (Herszenhorn and Stout 2008).

Contrast the 2008 farm bill process to the very next one—the 2014 farm bill. In 2011, when farm bill reauthorization discussions first began, the Republican-controlled House and Senate were aiming for a fiscally conservative approach to government. House Speaker John Boehner (R-OH) "declared his intent to end omnibus bills altogether," including the farm bill, and additionally pledged that any new spending would be offset with cuts elsewhere (Bosso 2017, 70). Bosso's book, *Framing the Farm Bill*, gives a detailed accounting of just how the 2012–2014 farm bill efforts went wrong. Many of its repeated failures and hiccups were related to a combination of partisan hardliners who were determined to slash government spending to the bone, as well as a lack of incentives for House leadership to act in a timely manner. Bosso also details the ways in which the farm bill got swept up in broader fights over the federal budget deficit during this time. Essentially, the farm bill got pulled into the broader partisan battle over spending and government size. During the two years (2012–2013) that the House struggled to bring a farm bill to the floor, the Senate was able to successfully pass not one but two compromise farm bills that had overwhelming support from both parties (though the majority of Senators who voted against the proposed legislation were Republicans, in spite of their own leadership's heavy hand in drafting the bill).

When Republican leaders brought the proposed farm bill to the House floor for a vote on June 20, 2013, House Majority Leader Boehner (R-OH) allowed the vote without first reaching a consensus within his own caucus and allowed nearly one hundred floor amendments to be considered in an effort to give the factions within the party the opportunity to be heard (Bosso 2017, 127). The legislation failed after a group of Democrats, joined by Tea Party Republicans, voted against the bill, for very different reasons. Democrats opposed the legislation for its cuts to nutrition spending, while Tea Party Republicans opposed it on the grounds that the estimated cost of the bill "is too big and would have passed welfare policy on the backs of farmers," as Marlin Stutzman (R-IN) told reporters (Abbott 2013). The failure was labeled as "shocking" and "embarrassing" in the news, which noted that this was the first farm bill to be voted down on the House floor in at least forty years (Abbott 2013). Interest groups expressed anger and frustration in response. The American Soybean Association, for example, issued a statement saying, "Today's failure leaves the entire food and agriculture sector in the lurch. Once again, the nation's soybean farmers and the 23 million Americans whose jobs depend on agriculture are left holding the bag" ("With Defeat of 2013 Farm Bill" 2013). Ultimately, in order to pass *any* kind of farm bill, House leaders, with Eric Cantor now at the helm, attempted to split the farm bill into two separate pieces of legislation—the Agriculture Reform, Food, and Jobs Act of 2013 (H.R. 2642), a "farm only" version of the Senate Farm Bill, and a nutrition bill titled the Nutrition Reform and Work Opportunity Act of 2013 (H.R. 3102), neither of which was acceptable to the Senate; instead, the House, on a party-line vote, adopted the Senate Bill as amended by their two bills, and agreed to send the entire thing to conference (Bosso 2017, 133). Perhaps because of this shocking series of events, the farm bill was the sixth most heavily lobbied bill, in dollars, of that year ("Bills: 2013" n.d.).

As the process of constructing the 2012–2014 farm bill illustrates, conflict over policy can potentially occur on two levels. First, conflict can occur between the parties and the extremes therein (polarization), and second, conflict can occur between interest groups lobbying for their preferred policy outcomes. But as these stories illustrate, the conflict was not driven by conflicting production sectors or regional disputes over commodity supports. In the case of the 2014 farm bill, the conflict between interest groups is not the driving source of conflict in agricultural policymaking; it was a reaction to the polarized nature of the policy realm. This chapter argues that political polarization is having drastic impacts on the behavior of interest groups and other policy advocates. To test these claims, the chapter relies on an expanded version of the dataset used in Chapter 3.[2]

SUBSYSTEM EXPANSION, INTEREST GROUP DENSITY

The agricultural subsystem has undoubtedly expanded over the decades, if we measure a subsystem by the number of interest groups involved. The volume of lobbying in agriculture, writ large, has increased in terms of both the number of active groups and the dollars spent on advocacy efforts (see Figure 5.1).

There is a clear relationship between the dollars spent on lobbying in the subsystem and the number of groups lobbying. Both (inflation adjusted) dollars spent and the number of lobbying groups increased between 1998 and 2013, with a few notable spikes. These spikes, as expected, occur around the years when Congress rewrote omnibus farm bills. Overall, it is

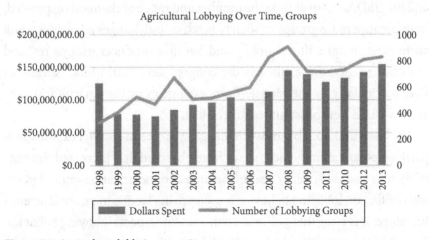

Figure 5.1 Agriculture lobbying over time, groups

clear that the agricultural subsystem is becoming more densely populated, both in and out of farm bill season.

Subsystem literature tells us that more competition in a subsystem drives interest groups to become specialists (find niches) in order to secure a competitive advantage with other groups (Baumgartner and Leech 2001; Browne 1990; Lowery et al. 2012). One congressional staffer I interviewed explicitly said that their office prefers when interest groups do not compete; they explained that they were more receptive to hearing from groups that "[spend] a lot less time throwing cold water on other people's proposals and [do] a better job of focusing, coming in, and talking about what they need."[3] If interest groups aren't necessarily competing more with each other, how do we explain the increased lobbying activity? Political polarization does a large part of the heavy lifting in that explanation.

CONFLICT EXPANSION, POLARIZATION, AND LOBBYING

Subsystem expansion is often driven by conflict expansion, which Schattschneider (1960) depicted as a dynamic whereby each side in a conflict recruits allies in order to prevail over the other. The agricultural subsystem, and others like it, once were able to damp down conflict by narrowing participation to producer interests and their allies in Congress and the USDA, but over time the number and range of claimants expanded, both because more groups in society (such as anti-hunger advocates) took an interest in agricultural policy and because producer groups realized that they needed more allies as the congressional "farm bloc" shrank in size, particularly in the House. Each expansion in the agricultural subsystem raised new possibilities for conflict.

The latest and possibly most challenging source of conflict expansion is partisan polarization, which, as we have observed, has increased dramatically over the past twenty years. The impact of polarization-rooted political conflict on lobbying behavior is a surprising lacuna in political science literature. It is clear that political environment impacts lobbying behavior, from the intensity with which groups lobby to the kind of groups that lobby

(Boehmke 2005; Dusso 2010; Plotnick and Winters 1990). However, if the relationship between political polarization and lobbying is understudied, it is not untouched. First, it is clear that there *is* a relationship. Various studies show that lobbying by non-profit interest groups actually *causes* increased polarization in Congress (Garlick 2021), as does lobbying by partisan think tanks (Fagan 2020). Another study, conducted at the state level, similarly found that polarization led to increased lobbying for non-profit organizations (Gray et al. 2015). Additionally, polarization has driven increased corporate lobbying efforts toward Congress (Brock 2021). These findings are complementary—together, they suggest a cycle of increasing polarization, which feeds lobbying activity, which then expands political conflict, encouraging further lobbying. I argue here that partisan *polarization causes increased lobbying* at the federal level, across both corporations and other interest groups.

Chapter 3 showed that partisan polarization has driven an increase in corporate lobbying. This chapter goes further to test this claim by expanding the analysis broadly among all types of interest groups across the agricultural subsystem. To do so, I use a negative binomial regression on the cross-sectional, time-series data of all interest groups across the time period.[4] The dependent variable is simply the total number of groups who reported actively lobbying during each year contained in the dataset. The independent variables, polarization, farm bill, divided congress, and number of hearings have been previously described in Chapter 3, and additional details can be found in Appendix A. Each of these independent variables represents a measure of agenda conflict or expansion that could help explain an increase in the number of groups lobbying over the time period.

Table 5.1 indicates that the increase in partisan polarization in Congress has had a significant impact on the number of groups lobbying the institution. Whether a farm bill is being considered in a given year also has a significant and positive impact on the number of groups lobbying, though the effect size is much smaller. Other measures of agenda expansion or conflict did not have a significant impact on the number of groups lobbying Congress. These results indicate that increased activity in lobbying over

Table 5.1 INCIDENT RATE RATIOS, NUMBER OF GROUPS
LOBBYING CONGRESS PER YEAR

Polarization	17.161**
	(2.843**)
Farm Bill	1.264*
	(0.234*)
Divided Congress	0.885
	(−0.123)
Number of Hearings	1.001
	(0.001)
Constant	10.820
	(2.381*)
N Log Likelihood	16
Wald Chi^2	−91.916
	41.59

NOTE: Coefficients appear in parentheses.

*$p < 0.05$; **$p < .01$

the course of the dataset can be at least partially attributed to conflict expansion driven by polarization. Polarization-linked conflict expansion not only generates subsystem expansion and leads to a greater number of lobbying groups; it also impacts how interest groups lobby within the subsystem.

INCREASES IN LOBBYING EFFORTS AMONG GROUPS

As Figure 5.1 illustrates, the number of groups engaged in lobbying between 1998 and 2013 steadily increased. Some of this reflects the general increase in lobbying, over time, in the United States. Lobbying is a self-perpetuating industry that expands for the sake of expansion, and it does so by capitalizing on the relative lack of information that businesses and interest groups possess about politics (Drutman 2015). Many businesses and interest groups believe the old adage, "If you aren't at the table, you're on the menu." Acquiring lobbyists and participating in politics is not only a matter of getting particularized benefits or extracting rents, in economics-speak. Lobbying is also, to put it bluntly, a matter of not getting eaten. Businesses, in particular, view lobbying as a form of insurance (LaPira and Thomas 2017).

That being said, lobbying as a defensive measure does not mean that it is not profitable. To the contrary, evidence suggests that lobbying can be extremely profitable (Alexander, Mazza, and Scholz 2009; Drutman 2015; Waterhouse 2015). Lobbyists, particularly revolving-door lobbyists, have deep process knowledge (LaPira and Thomas 2017) and can cue their clients to policy windows such as major regulatory reforms (Alexander, Mazza, and Scholz 2009) and budgeting discussions (de Figueiredo 2004), and are cognizant of the potential profitability of lobbying during these times.

I do not attempt to adjudicate the role of lobbying as insurance versus profit. Rather, I only argue that groups are lobbying more than ever before *as a consequence of political polarization.* This is not, however, to say that this is leading to "better" policy outcomes for lobbying groups. And as partisan polarization increases, legislative gridlock is sure to follow. This is particularly true when the House and Senate are controlled by different parties; intra-branch conflict is a leading source of policy inaction (Binder 1999). Partisan polarization and intra-branch conflict are inherently linked. If intra-branch conflict and gridlock are most likely to occur when the House and Senate are controlled by different parties, then as the parties move further from each other's ideal points through polarization, the conflict between them will naturally become exaggerated and more intense. Partisan polarization and intra-branch division are two sides of the same gridlocked coin.

Lobbying is already an exceptionally competitive endeavor, and there appears to be little connection between having money to pour into lobbying and gaining favorable policy outcomes (Baumgartner et al. 2009, 214). As partisan polarization slows the policy process and legislative gridlock increases, lobbying is sure to become a slower, more continuous process as well, requiring more resources to sustain over the long haul. It is not that resources have suddenly begun to better equate to policy outcomes. Rather, the activity of lobbying simply takes longer and requires more than ever before—more resources, more effort, and more time. I argue that groups must put in more effort for the same outcomes, whether that is profiting or simply not being "on the menu." In short, *interest groups in the agricultural sector must expend increasing effort on lobbying Congress as political polarization increases.*

I test this hypothesis essentially using the same methods and variables described in Chapter 3 and found in detail in Appendix A. In the following analysis, the dependent variable for each regression, respectively, is the number of lobbyists an interest group reported hiring to lobby Congress, the bureaucracy, or the White House, in a given year. In the interest of brevity, the dependent variable is referred to as "reports" of lobbying, by institution. Report counts are aggregated by interest group, each year. This provides me with a cross-sectional time-series dataset of lobbying interest groups from 1998 to 2013. There are a total of 2,817 interest groups who reported lobbying in agriculture during this sixteen-year time period, and the unit of analysis is interest group by year, yielding a total of 45,072 observations.

As illustrated in Figure 5.2, lobbying increased steadily, toward all institutions, during the time period included in the analysis. In order to test that it is truly polarization driving the increase in lobbying toward Congress, rather than simply an artifact of increased lobbying over time in general, I also look at lobbying directed toward the bureaucracy and the White House. If polarization is related to an increase in lobbying in Congress, but not toward the White House and bureaucracy, we can be fairly confident that it is political polarization that is driving the behavior change.

Here I perform a negative binomial regression on the cross-sectional, time-series data previously described.[5] In this chapter, like in Chapter 3, the number of lobbyists hired to work on agricultural lobbying is used as the best available proxy measure for the relative intensity of lobbying a group is engaging in at any given time. The independent variables used

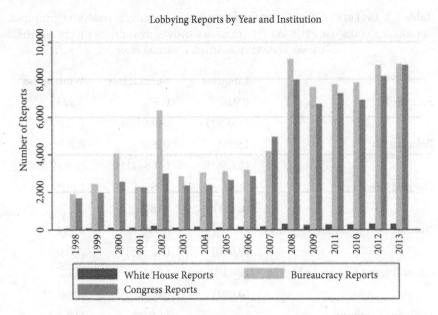

Figure 5.2 Lobbying reports by year and institution

here are a subset of those used in Chapter 4, given that there is much less information publicly available about many interest groups when compared with publicly traded firms. The analysis here relies on the following independent variables: polarization, divided congress, agricultural hearings, the number of other groups lobbying in a given year, and the lobbying activity that the interest group undertook in other venues.

LOBBYING A POLARIZED CONGRESS

The hypothesis predicted that polarization would drive increases in lobbying toward Congress, but not toward the bureaucracy or the White House, as lobbyists responded to a more "gridlocked" legislative environment. Table 5.2 confirms this hypothesis and suggests that there are additional resource-allocation decisions that interest groups may be making as a result of political polarization and intra-branch conflict (i.e., conflict expansion).

Table 5.2 INTEREST GROUP LOBBYING EFFORTS AS DIRECTED TOWARD CONGRESS, BUREAUCRACIES, AND THE WHITEHOUSE, AS SHOWN BY INCIDENT RATE RATIOS, USING NEGATIVE BINOMIAL REGRESSION

	Congress	Bureaucracy	Whitehouse
Farm Bill	0.926*	0.931	0.925
	(−.077*)	(−0.0715)	(−0.077)
Polarization	1.986*	0.188*	0.313
	(0.686*)	(−1.669**)	(1.161)
Divided Congress	1.042	1.083**	1.192*
	(0.041)	(0.805**)	(0.175*)
Number of Agriculture Hearings	1.000	0.995**	0.994
	(0.000)	(−0.005)**	(−0.006)
Other Interest Groups Lobbying	1.002**	1.002**	1.002**
	(0.002)	(0.002)**	(0.002**)
Lobbying Congress	–	1.064**	1.039**
		(0.062**)	(0.038**)
Lobbying Bureaucracy	1.021**	–	1.016**
	(0.021**)		(0.016**)
Lobbying White House	1.068**	1.161**	–
	(0.066**)	(0.149**)	
2007 Law Change	1.021	0.917	0.718**
	(0.021)	(−0.087)	(−0.332**)
Constant	0.022**	0.171**	0.137**
	(−3.834**)	(−1.766**)	(−1.984)
N	45,072	45,072	45.072
Log Likelihood	−51352.805	−41696.569	−5699.0619
Wald Chi²	3472.30**	9688.30**	859.66**

NOTE: Coefficients appear in parentheses.

$^*p < 0.05$; $^{**}p < .01$

The results in Table 5.2 confirm that interest groups in the agricultural sector have increased their lobbying toward Congress in response to partisan polarization, but not toward the White House or the bureaucracy. While the regression indicated a positive and significant relationship between political polarization and lobbying directed at Congress, there appears to be a negative and significant relationship between legislative polarization and lobbying activity directed toward bureaucracy. Groups may actually be shifting their resource allocation as a result of partisan conflict. At the same time, when the House and Senate are controlled by different parties (divided Congress), the results indicate that groups increase their efforts at lobbying the executive branch—both the White House and the bureaucracy—but they do not downshift their lobbying toward Congress during these periods.

The relationship between partisanship and increased lobbying is explored more in the following chapter, but before delving into that I want to answer the question, why don't interest groups downshift their lobbying toward Congress under conditions of divided partisan control? The short answer is because Congress ultimately remains in charge of writing (or not writing) the legislation that will impact their policy goals and their bottom lines. The story of how legislation to curb the marketing of unhealthy food to children did not come to pass is a quintessential example of why interest groups and corporations never relax their congressional lobbying efforts, even when the "action" might be centered in the executive branch or in agencies.

Under Democratic President Barack Obama, the early 2000s represented the height of public health concerns over obesity, health, and exercise in America. In 2009, Congress passed a measure asking that the Federal Trade Commission (FTC), the Centers for Disease Control and Prevention (CDC), the USDA, and the FDA create a working group, together, to draft new, voluntary standards for children's food marketing (Wilson and Roberts 2012). Shortly after, First Lady Michelle Obama launched the "Let's Move" campaign in 2010, with child health and obesity as a centerpiece of the administration's agenda. But in April 2012, Congress quietly killed the (congressionally requested) plan by the four federal agencies that targeted food marketing aimed at children. At the time, Republicans held the House, while Democrats controlled the Senate. The White House had been steadily pushing for improvements to school lunches (the Healthy, Hunger-Free Kids Act of 2010) and encouraging federal agencies to improve health guidelines and standards. In April 2011, the working group published its draft guidelines and food and beverage industries immediately mobilized, fearing that the proposed voluntary guidelines could become mandatory, killing their marketing efforts for many popular food products (Wilson and Roberts 2012).

Food and beverage industry groups lobbied heavily—targeting the White House, agencies, and Congress. They hired Anita Dunn, who was a former Obama White House Communications Chief, to run a new coalition called the Food Policy Coalition. This coalition of advocacy groups and corporations argued that the proposed voluntary guidelines would result in 75,000 lost jobs and nearly $29 billion in lost revenue (Wilson and Roberts 2012). Ultimately, though, their lobbying of Congress was what sealed the deal against the proposed guidelines. In a 130-page omnibus budget bill, Jo Ann Emerson (R-MO), chair of the appropriations subcommittee that funded the FTC, added a fifty-five-word sentence that single-handedly killed the inter-agency working group initiative (Wilson and Roberts 2012). The provision required that the group do a cost-benefit analysis of their proposed recommendations before finishing the report, a requirement that was prohibitively expensive and quietly ended the initiative to restrict corporate food marketing to children. The FTC later issued a statement saying, "Congress has clearly changed its mind about what it would like the Interagency Working Group to do with regard to the report on food marketed to children" (Wilson and Roberts 2012).

Additionally, Congress is ultimately in charge of directing the way that agencies implement laws, meaning that when agencies are unclear on how a particular provision of law should be implemented (especially if the law was written in ways that allow for considerable discretion), the agency, and the interest groups affected, may return to Congress to ask for clarification. One example comes from a menu labeling requirement that a lobbyist mentioned in one of our interviews. In the early days of implementation, after the passage of the Affordable Care Act, the Food and Drug Administration began developing guidance for which types of restaurants and retail establishments would be covered by the new requirements. FDA Commissioner Margaret Hamburg explained, "There are very, very strong opinions and powerful voices both on the consumer and public health side and on the industry side, and we have worked very hard to sort of figure out what really makes sense and also what is implementable," and described the implementation process as "extremely thorny" (Associated Press 2015). One particular point of confusion centered on whether the new provision applied more narrowly to restaurants only, or whether it encompassed *all* retail and restaurant establishments of a certain size. Ultimately, Congress had to clarify their intent:

> *The bill said . . . if you have twenty vending machines or more . . . or twenty restaurants or more, you have to post this information. Then the grocery stores and bowling allies and movie theaters questioned whether or not they would be covered. And they actually did not want to be covered because they don't think of themselves as restaurants. I recently saw where the people who authored that legislation, Congresswoman Rosa DeLauro and Senator Tom Harkin from Iowa, wrote a letter to the FDA saying, "Oh no, we did intend for the bowling allies and the grocery stores and the movie theaters to be covered. Let there be no mistake, we want them to be covered, we want this to be as broad as possible." So that's an example where someone could have gone to them to say, "We'd like you to clarify." It might have been public health, or they may have just done it on their own, I honestly don't know. We'd like you to clarify what you intended. . . . So, there would be times when you would go back to members of Congress. It doesn't mean that something is necessarily going to go that way, but it's a tool to clarify what Congress intended.[6]*

There is no stage of the legislative process, at the end of the day, in which Congress is not the ultimate statutory authority. These stories illustrate that, whether party control of Congress is divided or unified, and even when the locus of action appears to be with agencies, lobbyists continue to target Congress aggressively because of its oversight authority, its ultimate authority to enshrine preferences into statute (even when hamstrung by conflict), and its powerful ability to veto potentially undesirable outcomes. In the example of the proposed marketing guidelines, Congress did not need to rally and pass sweeping new legislation, nor did it need to unify behind policy change. Congress needed to do what comes so easily to it— exercise a veto point. This aligns with the wisdom that lobbying for the status quo can be financially worthwhile, particularly when the proposed alternative is potentially costly. On the other hand, in the case of menu regulations, members of Congress acted to clarify that the legislation that might have appeared vague in its broadness actually was intended to be broad and to encompass food vendors outside of the restaurant industry specifically.

CONFLICT EXPANSION INCREASES LOBBYING ACTIVITY

The evidence presented here suggests that conflict expansion compels individual interest groups to increase the number of lobbyists that they hire and put more effort into their advocacy in the agricultural subsystem. This analysis accounts for two possible forms of conflict expansion: that driven by polarization between the two parties and that driven by conflict between the House and Senate when they are controlled by opposing parties. In both cases, interest groups increase their lobbying efforts.

However, they do so in increasingly different ways. As de Figueiredo (2002) points out, interest groups often pursue a multi-venue strategy in their lobbying activities. For example, lobbyists increase the intensity of lobbying efforts toward the executive branch during times of intra-branch conflict, which makes sense when we consider the institutional dynamics of policymaking. Intra-branch conflict is one of the primary sources of gridlock in Congress (Binder 1999), and there is evidence that when the chambers are divided, bureaucracies may enjoy more administrative discretion, since the legislature may be unable to agree on detailed legislation

(Lowi, 1969; Huber, Shipan, and Pfahler 2001). Under these conditions, interest groups might reasonably find that they must expend more effort in the executive branch as some decision-making shifts in that direction. However, they do not stop lobbying Congress, particularly when administrative discretion veers into territory that a particular industry sector might not prefer. In these cases, a being prepared to lobby vociferously in all venues—agencies, Congress, and the White House—is essential to avoid being "on the menu."

Partisan polarization, however, exists independently of which party controls the House or the Senate. This ideologically based conflict is continually widening and is fundamentally changing the rules of the game within Congress, and in American government more generally. In the agricultural subsystem, in particular, polarization is wreaking havoc on the compromises between rural and urban lawmakers so historically essential to the construction and passage of farm bills, creating both high uncertainty and new opportunity (Good 2014; Neely 2013; Sheingate 2013). The next chapter digs more deeply into the underlying relationship between political polarization and increasingly intense efforts of lobbying interest groups.

6

He Said, She Said

The Power of Interest Group Negotiations

We have established that partisan polarization in Congress is altering the relationship between members of Congress and interest groups. Political environment clearly impacts interest group behavior, and increased polarization is an added feature that groups must navigate. More groups are lobbying Congress in response to conflict driven by polarization, and many groups have increased the volume of their lobbying toward Congress specifically. In short, party polarization in Congress is resulting in increased lobbying, conflict expansion, and more gridlock.

Polarization has disrupted the agricultural subsystem, which long had a unique reputation as a stable, cooperative, and conciliatory political environment in which lawmakers worked across party lines and where unusual coalitions flourished (Browne 1988, 1995; Hansen 1991; Sheingate 2003). However, polarization is rapidly changing relationships in Congress and destabilizing even the more long-standing and cross-cutting policy arenas (Good 2014; McCarty, Poole, and Rosenthal 2008; Sheingate 2013).

All of this has subtly shifted the role of advocacy groups in American politics. The interviews highlighted in this chapter reveal that the actors involved in the agricultural policy domain—both lobbyists and congressional staffers—often viewed the agricultural policy area as an example of unique cooperation, negotiation, and good policy process. Yet, in the same breath, many also noted the ways that polarization and uncertainty

Farmed Out. Clare R. Brock, Oxford University Press. © Clare R. Brock 2024.
DOI: 10.1093/oso/9780197683798.003.0006

were changing the political landscape. Here I consider how that disruption affects relationships inside the subsystem, and how that might in turn affect legislative outcomes. I argue that as long-standing coalitions between urban and rural lawmakers are shaken, interest groups increasingly insert themselves into the policy process, though the extent to which this results in substantive outcomes is unclear.

This chapter begins by exploring what academics already know about the interaction between lobbying, political environment, and policy outcomes. I then discuss how lobbyists, themselves, describe political polarization and their understanding of its impact on the industry.

MONEY, LOBBYING, AND POLICY OUTCOMES: THE ELUSIVE CONNECTION

Suggesting that financial resources are immaterial to an interest group's ability to influence policy outcomes is entirely counterintuitive. Our gut tells us that money *must* matter when it comes to influencing politics. No amount of research could persuade most of us otherwise. And yet, existing research often shows that lobbying does not have clear, predictable, or consistent connection to policy outcomes. As Baumgartner and his colleagues say, "for the most part, resources have no significant correlation with a positive policy outcome" (2009, 203). However, they find two notable exceptions: first, businesses with high levels of resources are slightly more likely to achieve their preferred policy goals; and, second, organizations with a high number of former covered officials, also known as "revolvers," are more likely to be successful in their lobbying efforts (Baumgartner et al. 2009, 203).

And undoubtedly there *is* a connection between money spent on politics and political outcomes (Koerth 2019; McKay 2020). Resources do not *always* create an advantage in achieving policy outcomes (Baumgartner et al. 2009), but neither are they immaterial. One way that money moderates political influence is in the form of startup costs. Lobbying is a costly activity, one that takes resources to even begin to engage in

(Austen-Smith and Banks 2000; Drutman 2015; Esteban and Ray 2006). However, once an organization has begun to engage in lobbying, the activity tends to be self-reinforcing. Organizations who pay attention to politics and choose to become involved have paid the startup costs; after this, the marginal costs of lobbying tend to decline and these organizations are likely to continue to lobby, or even increase their lobbying, because lobbying is "sticky" (Drutman 2015, 2). Once an interest group has sunk costs into the endeavor, it tends to find reasons to continue. Further, these organizations may begin to see the benefits to political engagement, both because their lobbyists convince them it is so and because there may be very real financial gain to be had from engagement (Alexander, Mazza, and Scholz 2009; Franklin 2014; LaPira and Thomas 2017).

As briefly discussed in Chapter 4, resources also matter because in lobbying they allow for compounded advantages to advocacy groups. The impact of interest group expenditures is more likely to appear in committee, rather than on the floor, and what these expenditures really impact is member enthusiasm and time (Hall and Wayman 1990). Amy McKay explores the relationship between campaign contributions, lobbying, and committee behavior in support of the finding that interest group money impacts legislator behavior at the committee level. Using plagiarism detection software, McKay shows that there is a clear relationship between amendments introduced by committee members and the fundraisers hosted by lobbyists; she finds highly similar, even identical language between letters from advocacy groups who hosted fundraisers and amendments introduced by committee members (2018).

At other times, lobbying may be a protective or precautionary activity (LaPira and Thomas 2017), meaning that negative lobbying—lobbying against change—may be just as important an activity as lobbying in favor of change. Take, for example, the industry's advocacy and Congress's subsequent murder of the 2012 inter-agency attempt to restrict food marketing targeting children (see Chapter 5). And, indeed, negative lobbying is often more successful since it is comparatively easier to convince Congress not to act than it is to convince it to do something (Baumgartner et al. 2009; McKay 2012). Whether lobbying for change or against it, sustained lobbying, session after session, does seem to be worth it over the long term—interest groups able to gain trust of policymakers may find themselves in a better position to help sway policy details or block unfavorable legislation (Hansen 1991).

So, the question of how resources influence policy outcomes, whether via campaign contributions, lobbying, or a combination of those activities, presents a thorny problem. There are nearly always groups lobbying for change and groups lobbying against change, and it becomes quite challenging to untangle the institutional preference for stasis and the role of partisan preferences from any influence that lobbying, or campaign contributions, might have on legislative outcomes. Added to this mess of nuance is the problem of understanding the counterfactual. We can essentially never observe what would have happened in the absence of lobbying on any given legislative battle.

Nonetheless, it is clear that money *does* matter. It may buy time and enthusiasm (Hall and Wayman 1990), it may increase the likelihood of favorable amendments in committee (McKay 2018, 2020), or it may facilitate sustaining long-term relationships that result in increased trust, and therefore influence, over time (Hansen 1991). But in all of these scenarios, lobbying is the primary means of converting money into influence.

The previous chapter showed that lobbying has increased under conditions of partisan polarization in Congress. Given that lobbying is a means of converting money to influence, through information transmission and persuasion, this raises two primary questions. First, how has polarization changed the political "playing field," especially for groups with fewer resources? And second, has increased lobbying, overall, resulted in increased influence? To understand these questions, we need to talk to participants themselves.

TALKING TO LOBBYISTS

This chapter is based on a set of twenty-four in-depth interviews conducted with lobbyists, legislative staffers, and reporters, many of whose words have already appeared in previous chapters.[1] Lobbyists were from corporations, producer associations, coalition and industry associations, contract companies, and labor unions. The purpose of these interviews was to establish how lobbyists say that they make strategic lobbying decisions, when they change strategies, and how their chosen strategies relate to their policy preferences and the political environment.

Interview subjects were first chosen randomly from a dataset of all lobbyists who worked on the 2008 farm bill. Subjects were contacted with an interview request via a mailed letter, then by email or phone. Further subjects were determined using "snowball sampling." That is, at the end of each interview, the subject was asked if he or she knew anyone else who might be willing to be interviewed on the subject, and those people were contacted. Additional subjects were those individuals who were key players during the 2008 farm bill, such as a senior legislative staffer for the then Chairman of the Senate Committee on Agriculture, Nutrition, and Forestry, and a staffer for the House Agriculture Committee.

All interviewees were asked a set of pre-determined questions; however, the conversation was free-form and allowed interviewees to steer the discussion. Interviews were recorded with permission and transcribed at a later date. No interviewee names are used in association with their comments, unless both explicitly permitted and deemed particularly useful to the narrative of the book.[2]

Interviews covered a range of topics, starting with the political landscape lobbyists faced, the topics they worked in, their opinions on the changing legal landscape regulating lobbyists, and more.

THE POLITICAL LANDSCAPE: DECLINING CONGRESSIONAL CAPACITY AND INCREASED DEMAND FOR INFORMATION

As discussed in Chapter 5, political environment impacts lobbying behavior. Studies suggest that environmental features such as uncertainty over outcomes (Dusso 2010) and party competition (Plotnick and Winters

1990) influence how interest groups lobby. Recent research adds increased partisan polarization and a related decline in institutional capacity as new features of the federal political environment in the United States. Through a decline in overall institutional capacity and through deliberate leadership action, rank-and-file members of Congress have ever less information and less influence over the content of legislation (Curry 2015). A lobbyist who worked on the Hill at one time explained, "When I first started in this business in the 1980s, the staff on the agriculture committees, they were professional staff. They provided analysis. It was not Democrat or Republican. And they provided it to both sides. That would be unheard of today."[3]

At the same time as staff support for members of Congress has shrunk (Reynolds 2021), the fundraising and constituency demands on members' time have steadily increased. Members are spending more time than ever dialing for dollars and doing constituency work (Klein 2013). They also must use what time they have left to deal with increasingly complex topics and thorny regulatory problems as our society is transformed by technology and modern life. In short, members of Congress spend less time on legislating and are increasingly consumed by the "perpetual campaign," which forces them to devote ever-increasing time to winning majority status, and inevitably shrinks time spent on legislating (Lee 2016). This perpetual campaign also feeds the ideological gulf between the parties and exacerbates partisan polarization (Lee 2016).

Interest groups tend to interact with partisan politics differently, depending on their type. Groups that align themselves with political parties are distinct in their motivations and behaviors from those that do not (Fagan, McGee, and Thomas 2021). Additionally, interest groups that emphasize lobbying (as opposed to electioneering through campaign contributions) are more likely to be bipartisan and less ideological than their counterparts (Tripathi, Ansolabehere, and Snyder 2017). Within the agricultural sector, most groups fall into the categories of trade associations, corporate lobbyists, and coalition groups, all of which prefer *not* to align too closely with one or another party. In interviews, lobbyists often bemoaned partisan polarization and the impact it has had on the agricultural policy space. One lobbyist noted the combined problem of partisan polarization and perpetual campaigning: "The lack of bipartisanship, the lack of trust, and members going back every weekend [means that] the relationships or the depth of relationships are just not there. . . . The willingness to work together across the aisle has declined."[4] Beyond this, the *ability* of members to coordinate and work together has perhaps declined as members have increasingly less time spent in each other's company. Even the famous "Alpha House," where some of the nation's most powerful Democratic lawmakers (including George Miller (D-CA), Charles E. Schumer (D-NY), and Richard Durbin (D-IL)) resided for more than three decades, has closed its doors and was sold to a restaurateur.

One might conclude that between the broadening of government and declining institutional capacity, the informational subsidy lobbyists can provide would be more in demand than ever before (Hall and Deardorff 2006). In this environment, lobbyists serve as a conduit for indirect communication, bridging the ideological divide, and negotiating between the parties and members of Congress (Andres 2009). Polarization increases congressional reliance on the services of lobbyists. Lobbyists can, and do, act as go-betweens for congressional offices. As Andres (2009, 116) notes, "Lobbyists fill the vacuum created by partisanship. Polarization has strengthened their hand in a process where information—particularly intelligence about what is happening on the other side of the aisle—is a highly valuable commodity."

So, what does this all mean for lobbyists? They're working harder than ever before and the information they provide is more valuable to legislators and staff. But, at the same time, legislators engaged in the perpetual campaign have less time to work on legislation, or even to be physically present on the Hill. There is less readily available face-to-face time between lobbyists and legislators. This also means that lobbyists have had to change their tactics and strategies for contacting legislators:

Technology has changed it a lot. In a prior lobbying life . . . the old adage goes, you better be wearing out a lot of shoe leather on Capitol Hill. Lobbyists would literally just . . . their office was the halls of

Congress, every day up there walking around, seeing who they can meet, grabbing somebody going and getting a cup of coffee, hanging outside their office when they come out. That was lobbying 101. Don't do that today. If you go up to Congress you don't see lobbyists just hanging out, shuttling back and forth in the halls. . . . It's all done via email. My staff have great email and social media relationships with the staff on Capitol Hill, and that's the way they prefer it to operate. They're . . . that personal nature of it, is not there anymore.[5]

Similarly, another lobbyist said:

I think overall it was better, relationships were stronger and there was less miscommunication that sometimes happens electronically because people are just dashing off messages. I don't know. I would say, we used to spend oodles of time when we'd write a letter to Congress actually delivering it. Now we just push a button, and they all get it. The difference being, when you're actually delivering it and putting it in someone's hand, you're also having verbal communication that's going on. So, obviously now it's so much quicker and it's more efficient in some ways. Ultimately, I'm not sure that the old way wasn't better.[6]

For this reason, among lobbyists, connections are more valuable than subject matter expertise. Deep process knowledge and strong relationships are much rarer than substance knowledge (Bertrand, Bombardini, and Trebbi 2014; LaPira and Thomas 2017). In this regard, lobbyists tend to come in two varieties: revolvers and subject matter experts. Revolvers have spent time on the Hill as staffers, or even as members. Subject matter experts are more likely to have worked in the field that they now represent as a lobbyist. Revolving-door lobbyists are highly sought after because there are comparatively fewer of them, and they tend to possess connections that subject-matter experts do not. If lobbyists were only providing information to members of Congress, expertise *should* actually be more valuable than process knowledge, or at least as valuable. This, of course, is not the case because interest groups are still hoping to influence policy content—not just to provide free information with nothing in return. The value placed on process over substance knowledge indicates that there is something about the combination of the shortage of time and attention in Congress, along with the evolving congressional environment, that is increasing the value of process knowledge.

PROVIDING AIR COVER AND NEGOTIATION: COALITION BUILDING AS A NEGOTIATION SUBSIDY

So, lobbyists are not providing *only* informational subsidies for members of Congress. In fact, information is overabundant in today's modern media and internet landscape. However, that doesn't mean that it is the specific type of information that members of Congress need. While lobbyists have always provided informational subsidies to legislators (Hall and Deardorff 2006), their role has morphed to include a type of *negotiation subsidy*. Members of Congress, increasingly left in the dark about policy details (Curry 2015), need reliable information about how legislation will be received with constituents back home, relevant industries, and with their co-partisans outside of Congress. Interest groups can provide valuable cues regarding how legislation will be received, communicate between offices, and help provide political cover to members of Congress.

While individual lobbyist strategies varied depending on specific issues, personal preference, and personal brand, some common threads emerge from interviews. Lobbyists report being aware and strategic regarding which legislators they approach, and when and how they approach advocacy. Almost all lobbyists emphasized the importance of finding legislative champions,[7] but also the importance of not assuming that legislative offices are communicating correct information with each other, if at all. Multiple lobbyists reported directly asking their champions to speak with certain other members of Congress, such as the committee chair,[8] or to other specific offices.[9] Another lobbyist discussed at length working with a minority leader (a Democrat) on particular legislation; the lobbyist specifically worked with that legislator to communicate to Republicans how many votes the minority member believed that he would be able to deliver, depending on a particular provision. This lobbyist explained:

> I talked to him personally, and he said he can deliver about eighty Democrats for the farm bill. . . . But he says he doesn't know how many he can deliver, if any, if there were big cuts. So, he's trying to get that across to the Republicans that he wants Democrats supported. You got to keep that together. So that's scaring us that's all . . . polarization is rearing its ugly head for us right now. It [We are] just trying to help communicate that message.[10]

This theme—lobbyists explicitly trying to carry and coordinate messages between offices—continued, as another lobbyist explained, "You shouldn't assume that the offices are talking to each other; you need to make sure that you know your messages are being communicated. You need to go out there and talk to each office, individually, so they share information."[11] Lobbyists were careful, however, to clarify that they weren't telling members of Congress how to do their jobs. One lobbyist explained this rather fine line:

> I might try to get a particular member to better understand a perspective . . . or I might tell their staff, "Hey you might want to reach out to this other office; I think [they] may be able to help better explain it or better facilitate connection." [But] I don't tell members what to do. Ever. If I have any relation with that staffer, I might tell them, "You might want to talk to so-and-so, or your boss might want to; because I think their perspective might be helpful." But I'll let them carry that forward. . . . And I would say particularly when you are working with the committee staff, they might want to know, "Well, have you talked to so-and-so or do you know what's this person thinking?"[12]

Another lobbyist described their job as being "very much behind the scenes." They often help members "work with their colleague[s]," including helping members work with colleagues who are the same party but who see things differently, with the hope that the lobbyist can "maintain the support of this member but also bring somebody else"; in other words, they view their role as "facilitating members working together."[13]

Lobbyists describe working harder to act as go-betweens and negotiators as members of Congress, and particularly the House, have become less collegial. They specifically identify partisan polarization as a source of increased advocacy workload. In particular, lobbyists report what Curry explains in *Legislating in the Dark*; leadership increasingly is taking over the details of legislation, leaving rank-and-file members entirely out of the process (Curry 2015). One lobbyist said, "There is no consistent schedule for how these spending bills you're to get done, and so it becomes a free-for-all where the committee then starts to lose control of what's in their bill because the congressional leadership is trying to determine what's going to be in it."[14]

Simply put, lobbyists believe that their job is getting harder. One defense against the increasing gridlock and conflict is coalition work. Coalitions, in particular, support the need for negotiation. Cross-partisan or "unholy alliance" coalitions particularly help reduce friction by disarming potential partisan opponents. One lobbyist described frustration at the increasingly gridlocked nature of Congress. He described coalitions among interest groups as providing political, partisan "air cover," but expressed a concern that such air cover was increasingly needed for passing even the simplest legislation. Speaking about a historically bipartisan and popular policy that was up for renewal, the lobbyist vented, "but this shouldn't be something where I have to build a coalition to provide the air cover. Members like coalitions, they want the air cover. [But now] it's air cover for things you really need."[15]

The negotiation subsidy that lobbyists are providing, therefore, does not necessarily mean that a lobbyist is walking into an office saying, "Senator *X* wants this, and Senator *Y* wants this other thing, and so we suggest this compromise." As an earlier quote illustrated, such a bold move would likely be received poorly. Rather, lobbyists and the interest groups they represent are doing a lot of the work of negotiating between various interests and stakeholders, forming coalitions, and trying to reduce outside opposition to legislation. In doing so, they provide cover to legislators and make it easier for members of Congress to support legislation—especially given that the rank-and-file members may have ultimately had very little hand in crafting the contents of the proposed bill.

Indeed, a lot of lobbying has always taken place in coalitions. "Lobbying also often takes place within coalitions, making it important to measure the efforts of all allied groups rather than that of any single group," Baumgartner and Leech argue. "Any model that does not take into consideration the effects of indirect lobbying and coalitional behavior is likely to be under-specified" (Baumgartner and Leech 1998, 139). And such lobbying tends to be more effective than lone-voice efforts. As Baumgartner and Leech explain, "members of Congress listen to organizations when they think the organizations may end up putting together a coalition that cannot be ignored. The social nature of lobbying, with its sensitivity to context, can therefore be characterized by mimicry, cue-taking, and bandwagoning effects" (1998, 140). This mirrors exactly what lobbyists themselves believe about their coalitional efforts.

Lobbyists form industry coalitions that appeal across the partisan aisle, and in doing so they provide political cover for members of Congress to support emerging compromises. Indeed, coalition building was described to take up an increasing amount of time for lobbyists, and to be increasingly vital to their success. "What we've found . . . on addressing issues is that the days of the lone voice are over. So, we manage or run more than one alliance or coalition. We've built these things— that's become our specialty. Managing a coalition or managing a group of people is very difficult."[16] That managing a coalition successfully *is* in fact, very difficult, seemed to be a consensus more broadly. Another lobbyist explained, "There was one [coalition] around the farm bill in 2008 where we actually had ground rules. And one of the ground rules was, you can disagree, but you can't harm the other person's initiative. And I thought it was a really good ground rule, but it's incredibly difficult to enforce."[17]

These groups have the right idea, according to a legislative staffer, who talked about the united front that they prefer to see from lobbyists.

A united message is more persuasive, effective, and likely to be successful, and the broader the coalition behind the message, the better:

> *The model that we always point to is the sugar industry; they have cane farmers and processors; they have sugar beet farmers. And they all come together, and they fight a lot behind closed doors. And then [they come together on] policy and no one talks about disagreements. They hit the Hill and they are very consistent. Not all organizations are like that. You know some, you have different stakeholder organizations that kind of defect from whatever their policy is, which I—but I get. You know you got to advocate what works best for your actual members. But I think that the way to be successful is to have all those disagreements behind closed doors and then have a unified message whenever you come up here.*[18]

Ideally, lobbyists report that they target their coalitional strategy to the partisanship in Congress. "You tune your coalition to align with the political composition of Congress to the best of your ability."[19] These coalition groups are deliberately looking to provide political cover to partisans, and allow them to take a vote or support a policy that might otherwise be challenging:

> *We try to come together with a strategy on some specific issues that some [policymakers] might feel a little more delicate about or that might make some people recoil initially if they don't have an in-depth of knowledge on it. You try to find another group or coalition that people might be more inclined to trust. You try to have them understand how the issue is important and how it impacts them, then educate them to the point that they can communicate.*[20]

Groups also have to be flexible and quick to adjust to the changing political environment; and some groups, depending on the issues they focus on, will have to be more adaptable than others. One lobbyist discussed the importance of adapting quickly to changing political priorities, "but we do have to be more nimble now and alter our arguments on how to sustain the support of conservatives."[21] Another lobbyist said, "Yeah, if you can hold hands with a group that may not be perceived as a traditional partner with industry[, it] provides a lot of credibility to the issue."[22]

At the same time as coalitions provide cover for politicians to make potentially challenging decisions, they also provide the groups with a different type of political cover. In a coalition, interest groups are less likely to be pressed to affiliate with one partisan side or another, and this helps them protect the integrity of their message against partisan attacks. When a group can achieve unity ("coalition unity is certainly critical"[23]) and stay on message, it can be an important defensive strategy: "I think it's becoming increasingly important because it's increasingly difficult to get meaningful legislation through Congress because there are so many opportunities to move members on these issues, and messages can get distorted so quickly."[24]

In short, partisanship is not only increasing the amount of lobbying on Capitol Hill, it is also forcing lobbying to become more cooperative, "politically diverse,"[25] and coalitional. As the political landscape has shifted, interest groups have adapted. And coalitions are not only useful in lobbying Congress. Research shows that organizationally diverse coalitions, in particular, are more effective at lobbying bureaucracies for preferred outcomes; in the case of bureaucracy, unlike Congress, bipartisan coalitions matter much less (Dwidar 2022). This suggests that to be truly successful, organizations must adapt and be strategically savvy, lobbying in bipartisan coalitions when approaching Congress, while changing strategies to focus on organizational diversity when targeting bureaucracies.

All this also means that interest groups have to step up their lobbying activities, sustain them for longer, and pour more effort into them. Partisanship and gridlock, deteriorating relationships between members of Congress, and rising electoral demands on legislator time, have together generated a new and rockier political environment that interest groups are forced to navigate. Groups report being increasingly concerned with providing political cover and coalitional support, both to members of Congress and to themselves; indeed, they report that this is becoming almost necessary for any kind of success in advocacy.

There are important implications for interest groups being required to sustain lobbying efforts over longer time periods, multiple Congresses and changing political contexts, and through bitter partisan fights. As one lobbyist described it, "It's like Groundhog Day. You're going back and talking about the same issue [repeatedly], and back again next year with this issue."[26] We turn to those implications next.

7

Money, Money, Money

The Link between Influence and Wealth

Lobbying is expensive. However, once a group has overcome the high startup costs, lobbying quickly becomes a self-reinforcing activity (Drutman 2015). Yet, puzzlingly, wealth on its own is not a clear or decisive advantage in securing policy outcomes (Baumgartner et al. 2009; McKay 2012). One reason may be the decidedly status-quo bias of the political system. It is not that wealth does not impact success, it is that wealth is outshone by the propensity of Congress to do nothing. Overall, being a defender of the status quo is the best predictor of lobbying success (Baumgartner et al. 2009).

The congressional bias toward status quo has not deterred lobbying. Partisan polarization and the resulting gridlock are symptoms of conflict expansion in Congress (Binder 1999; Layman et al. 2010). Conflict expansion, in turn, increases opportunities for political activity by outsiders (Baumgartner and Jones 1993; Schattschneider 1960). In Chapter 6, I argued that while conflict expansion increases lobbying activity, polarization has also lengthened the lobbying time horizon and created new opportunities for interest groups to influence legislation. Now, I consider the policy implications of the combination of a lengthened political timeline due to gridlock, combined with increased informational and negotiation subsidies from interest groups.

Farmed Out. Clare R. Brock, Oxford University Press. © Clare R. Brock 2024.
DOI: 10.1093/oso/9780197683798.003.0007

In agriculture, the policy stakes are high: the outcomes of federal agriculture policy influence everything from our diets to our water quality (Davis and Brock 2020). As Americans, our very health and well-being are subtly influenced by subsidies and grants doled out through the farm bill. For businesses and organized interests in the agricultural sector, the potential opportunities for rent seeking are numerous. Discretionary programs include farm support, research and education programs, commodity and income support programs, crop insurance, farm loan programs, food aid, and livestock and meat marketing protection initiatives (Committee on the Budget 2018). Additionally, the farm bill funds a variety of environmental and sustainability programs. In other words, for interest groups and corporations who engage in lobbying, the farm bill offers myriad opportunities to carve out some slice of the pie.

Such opportunities extend beyond the large sums of money divvied up and distributed through various farm bills. The policy domain also includes a robust regulatory structure that (ideally) protects us from foodborne illness, monitors our drinking water, creates dietary guidelines, and determines the cafeteria lunches of children from Portland, Maine, on one coast to Portland, Oregon, on the other. These regulations and restrictions have everyday implications for our health, our wallets, and our waistbands. More broadly, issues like climate change and technological advances are also altering the food and agriculture landscape in ways that are often ambiguous and ill defined, proverbial "wicked" problems that require a degree of expertise beyond the grasp of most members of Congress, or their staff. Added uncertainty over problem definition and regulatory authority creates new challenges for governance, and often forces Congress to look to witness testimony, bureaucrats, and others to grapple with newly presented governance challenges (Lewallen 2020).

THE AGRIBUSINESS WEALTH GAP

So far, we have established a relationship between the changing partisan climate in Washington, DC, and the volume of lobbying that interest groups in the agricultural sector engage in. Partisan polarization increases gridlock and has increased legislative delay (Binder 1999; Hughes and Carlson 2015), and the upshot is a lengthened legislative process that forces interest groups and corporations seeking to sway policy to be ready to sustain their lobbying efforts over a longer time horizon, a problem about which lobbyists are well aware. High-salience, must-pass legislation, like the farm bill, generally does make it through the legislative process, albeit with much conflict and angst, and often over a longer time frame with higher risk of initial failure. Lower salience legislation, even legislative renewals that were once comparatively easy to pass, more often become a casualty of a gridlocked and bitterly partisan process. One lobbyist described how smaller pieces of legislation that were once a given for renewal are now more likely to face obstruction: "I find the issues that should have been a lighter lift have become a Herculean lift," the lobbyist explained. "The [volume] of noise and distractions is so much different now."[1] This indicates that for many interest groups the role of "adjunct staffer" brings the benefit of potentially increased influence over policy, but at the cost of more expensive advocacy and less timely congressional action.

The lengthening of the legislative process (Hughes and Carlson 2015), decline of congressional capacity (Curry 2015; Lewallen 2020), and increased complexity of legislation have created an environment in which resources matter more than ever (Drutman 2015, 3). This reality creates a gap between lobbying interest groups, in which the established "advantage of business" (Lindblom 1980) has expanded. Indeed, even within the business community, there appears to be a widening gap between relatively wealthier and poorer firms.

This chapter returns to the agribusiness and corporate lobbying dataset[2] from Chapter 4. The data are organized by firm-year, meaning that revenue and lobbying behavior are recorded for each firm, during each year from 1998 to 2013, generating a total of 4,992 observations. Here, I return to the relationship between lobbying and revenue. Chapter 4 showed a clear relationship between firm revenue and lobbying activity; agribusiness corporations with increased revenue also expanded their lobbying

Table 7.1 REPORTS OF LOBBYING BY INSTITUTION

	Lobbying Congress	Lobbying Bureaucracy	Lobbying White House
Low Revenue	0.844**	0.764**	0.012**
(N = 2,499)	(0.059)	(0.066)	(0.003)
High Revenue	3.011**	3.100**	0.166**
(N = 2,493)	(0.156)	(0.184)	(0.017)

NOTE: $N = 4,992$. Standard errors appear in parentheses.

*$p < 0.05$; **$p < .01$

activity. When considering *only* the scale of revenue and the amount of lobbying an agricultural firm reports engaging in, the relationship between the two variables is statistically significant, if somewhat weakly correlated.[3] But, splitting firms at the median normalized revenue and running a *t*-test shows that firms with higher than median revenue engage in significantly more lobbying than firms whose revenue is at or below the median reported revenue.

For all the reported tests, the null hypothesis is rejected. Confirming the regression evidence from Chapter 4, the *t*-tests in Table 7.1 demonstrate that firms reporting a higher-than-median revenue are significantly more likely to engage in lobbying at every level of government compared to those firms who report revenue at or below the median. This finding among firms lobbying on agricultural issues corroborates the conventional wisdom that lobbying is expansive and that engaging in it requires considerable access to resources. We can also observe this trend using a basic two-way scatter plot of revenue and the total amount of lobbying firms report engaging in, by year.

As Figure 7.1 demonstrates, the relationship between lobbying activity and resources has become more exaggerated over time.[4] The lobbying gap between firms reporting higher revenue and those reporting lower revenue is becoming steadily more exaggerated. When lobby reporting laws in 2007 increased the frequency of reporting from two times annually to quarterly, the effects are reflected in a bump in the amount of

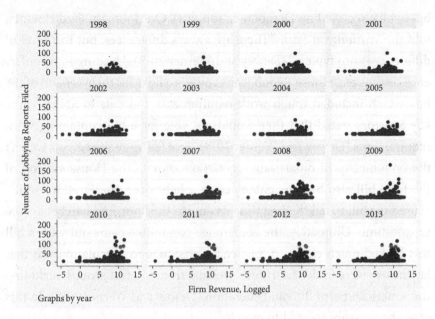

Figure 7.1 Relationship between lobbying reports and firm revenue, by year

lobbying reported among higher revenue firms, but, noticeably, not for lobbying reported by lower revenue firms. And between 2009 and 2013, the peakedness of the distribution skews increasingly heavily to the left. Resources clearly allow firms to engage in politics more aggressively.

The agricultural policy landscape and political environment in which these high-revenue firms are engaging more heavily was also becoming more dramatically partisan during this same time period. Chapter 4 described the devolution that shifted agricultural policy in the early 2000s from a bipartisan policy area that tended toward regional divides (as illustrated by Congress, not once but twice overcoming a presidential veto to pass the farm bill), to a bitter partisan battlefield in 2013, in which the House struggled to pass any legislation at all and was forced to resort to creative methods to move legislation to conference committee. Even in 2018, passage was no easier; even under conditions of unified government, with a GOP-controlled Congress and White House. The Senate version of the bill, which required support from Democrats to meet the sixty-vote threshold, was dramatically different from the House version of the bill (which received no Democratic support). One lobbyist, Ferd Hoefner, told the *Washington Post*, "There are always differences, but this level of difference is not typical" (Dewey and Werner 2018). Heading into conference committee, House Republicans vowed to fight for their version of the bill, which included tough work requirements and cuts to SNAP, while key Senators stated that they would not vote for a bill containing work requirements (Dewey and Werner 2018). And SNAP requirements weren't the only hiccup in bipartisan negotiation efforts. The House version of the farm bill also became entangled in a fight over immigration, which caused the bill to fail the first time it came to the floor, and barely pass the second time. Ultimately, the conference committee came out with a bill that looked much closer to the Senate version, and speculation was that lawmakers were under enormous pressure from interest groups, including the American Farm Bureau Federation (Dewey and Werner 2018). In this case, the pressure seemed to matter.

IN-HOUSE VERSUS REVOLVERS: WHO GETS HIRED BY WHOM?

More time means more money in lobbying, generally speaking, but not all lobbying is created equal. While interest groups are presumably created with the express purpose of political advocacy, the same is not true of corporations, for which deciding to engage in political advocacy entails high fixed startup costs. However, as Drutman notes, "once companies invest, there are decreasing marginal costs to additional political activity" (Drutman 2015, 132). In other words, as corporations become increasingly invested in political advocacy, they can begin to function (in the political space) slightly more like interest groups.

More frequent lobbying and a larger resource pool mean expanded strategic options for advocacy (Drope and Hansen 2006). While interest groups are most likely to lobby their co-partisans and allies in Congress to subsidize their legislative efforts (Hall and Deardorff 2006), groups with a "strong resource base" are able to expand their support by lobbying undecided committee members and even opponents (Hojnacki and Kimball 1998, 775). Lobbying may not buy these legislators' votes, but it does impact the likelihood that preferred legislation will make it onto the legislative agenda (Butler and Miller 2021).

As corporations begin to function more like interest groups by engaging in continual legislative monitoring and activity, they can make more effective lobbying choices. In-house lobbyists are much "cheaper" by the hour than contract lobbyists (LaPira and Thomas 2017). In-house lobbyists are often information oriented and can offer expertise and substantive clarity to members of Congress dealing with complex policy (Baumgartner and Jones 2015; Esterling 2004; LaPira and Thomas 2017). They can keep a more constant eye on legislation in Congress and alert their employer to any activity of interest. Contract lobbyists, who are often revolvers and have deeper political connections than subject matter expertise, also come at a premium price tag (Bertrand, Bombardini, and Trebbi 2014) but are hired as needed rather than employed 365 days a year. Corporations that possess a large budget for political engagement can rely on in-house lobbyists to monitor the legislative agenda and provide subject matter expertise, then outsource to contract lobbyists on those occasions when circumstances demand connections and legislative process knowledge.

Corporations engaging in political advocacy therefore have three primary options for lobbying. Some will opt not to lobby with any regularity and will hire a contract lobbyist for one-off opportunities when they wish to engage;[5] some will rely on in-house lobbyists to engage in frequently lobbying and legislative monitoring; and some will rely on in-house lobbyists and contract lobbyists. The most common activity, regardless of the type of lobbyist a firm relies on, is to not lobby at all. This comports with what we know in the literature and from interviews: it is hard to get things done in Congress, and often lobbyists are just watching and monitoring what is happening with the assumption that the status quo is more likely to prevail (Baumgartner et al. 2009). One lobbyist said, in reference to an unfavorable potential tax bill, "We're keeping our head low on that. We're watching it, and we're ready to go very public if that were to happen, but our tactic right now is just let them do what they want to do, and we're gonna keep quiet. Because we don't think Congress is ready to deal with any tax legislation at this point, so why stir the pot?"[6]

Groups that prefer the status quo will only lobby if it becomes absolutely necessary to do so. But, as one lobbyist said, "at the end of the day, agriculture has a lot to defend."[7] The other three options, moving beyond watchful waiting—hiring a contract lobbyist, using an in-house lobbyist, or using both an in-house and contract lobbyist—are all departures from the status quo of watchful waiting. And the ability of a corporation to engage, and the type of engagement they choose, will heavily depend on political conditions and the resources it has available.

This raises a series of questions: Which firms employ in-house lobbyists; when do firms hire contract lobbyists; and under what conditions will a firm that already has an in-house lobbyist also hire a contract lobbyist?

I use a multinomial logit to assess how corporations in the agricultural policy space will choose from lobbying strategies, relying on the previously described business-group dataset of 277 corporations lobbying between 1998 and 2013. The dependent variable here is lobbyist strategy: whether a corporation used an in-house lobbyist, a contract lobbyist, or both.[8] The base strategy for comparison is engaging in no lobbying at all, which corporations chose 3,760 times over the course of the 4,992 observations in the dataset. Over that same time period, corporations chose to use in-house lobbyists alone to engage in lobbying a total of 396 times, to rely on a contract lobbyist alone 707 times over the course of the time period, and to use both an in-house and contract lobbyist 129 times (see Figure 7.2). When firms move from watchful waiting to action, their decisions regarding what type of lobbyist strategy to use—in-house, contract, or both—are presumably both strategic and constrained. Firms respond to the perceived risk or reward of particular legislation, but they are also constrained by their own financial and budgetary concerns, the preferences of their board members, and perhaps the decisions they have made in the past concerning lobbying.

As Figure 7.3 indicates, more lobbying tends to occur during years in which farm bills were passed and the year preceding passage, during which they were deliberated. This aligns with evidence from previous

Money, Money, Money

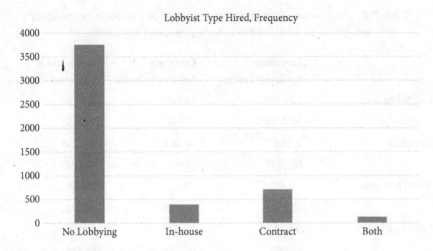

Figure 7.2 Lobbyist-type strategy used by firms

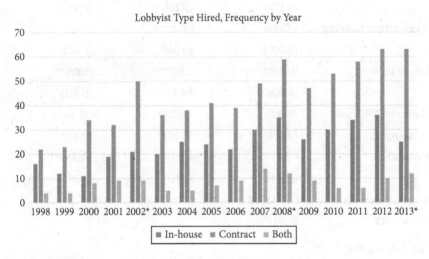

Figure 7.3 Lobbyist type hired, excluding the choice not to lobby, by year (*Note.* *Asterisks indicate years during which a farm bill was passed, with the caveat that the 2013 farm bill was passed during the first days of January of 2014)

chapters. Additionally, however, more firms lobby using *both* a contract and an in-house lobbyist.[9]

Table 7.2 shows that wealthier corporations are more likely to hire in-house lobbyists. The results also indicate that a corporation is more likely to lobby (with any strategy) when other firms are lobbying, confirming

Table 7.2 MULTINOMIAL LOGISTIC REGRESSION OF CORPORATE LOBBYIST
STRATEGY IN AGRICULTURE, BASE STRATEGY NO LOBBYING

	In-House Lobbyist Coeff.	Contract Lobbyist Coeff.	In-House & Contract Coeff.
Lag lobbyist strategy	1.369**	1.879**	3.223**
	(0.069)	(0.061)	(0.165)
Revenue	0.084**	−0.026	−0.058
	(0.024)	(0.019)	(0.041)
Farm bill year	−0.185	−0.112	−0.110
	(0.226)	(0.203)	(0.436)
Polarization	0.820	−0.677	−0.916
	(0.900)	(1.713)	(3.526)
Divided Congress	0.125	0.287*	0.498
	(0.159)	(0.141)	(0.293)
Agriculture hearings	−0.005	−0.003	0.008
	(0.007)	(0.006)	(0.013)
Firms lobbying	0.016**	0.017**	0.029**
	(0.006)	(0.005)	(0.011)
Dummy 2007 law change	−0.102	−0.090	−0.464
	(0.226)	(0.204)	(0.429)
Constant	−5.044	−2.995*	−7.899**
	(1.571)	(1.411)	(0.293)
Log Likelihood	−2770.335		
Pseudo R2	0.261		

NOTE: $N = 4{,}992$.

$^*p < 0.05$; $^{**}p < .01$

the bandwagoning effect in lobbying behavior that other scholars have observed. While revenue is significant in predicting the decision to hire an in-house lobbyist, it is not significant for choosing the strategy of hiring both an in-house and a contract lobbyist. This is puzzling at face value, since revenue is significant for the use of an in-house lobbyist and hiring both an in-house and a contract lobbyist is predicated on first making the decision to employ an in-house lobbyist, then to add onto that lobbying power. One explanation may be that most corporations are not that politically savvy. Their employees may not fully understand the differences between in-house and contract lobbyists, or they may simply rely on what their in-house lobbyists tell them regarding politics. Drutman explains, "This is a classic principal–agent problem, with corporate managers acting as agents and lobbyists acting as principals. Corporate managers hire lobbyists to deliver political benefits . . . [and] because politics is highly uncertain and ambiguous, lobbyists benefit from a powerful information asymmetry. Companies depend on lobbyists to interpret politics for them, and advise them on strategy" (2015, 6).

However, another possible explanation came from a lobbyist who runs a contract firm. He explained that companies often hire his firm because they cannot afford a continual presence:

> *The full-time employee, that means benefits, that means infrastructure, office, that sort of thing. Some of them, I think, look at us as a value prop. If they were going to hire me individually it would probably be at a level that's not in their budget. So, they're able to hire some of our time and get a return that maybe exceeds that of what they would get if they had someone on their payroll. They hire us because, with our experience and our networks, we also bring more than just one person. Let's just say that you have a client who pays you $10k a month, so $120 thousand dollars, but they're getting the whole team, so they're getting a lot of different aspects. They're getting high-level contacts, intellectual capital, they're getting hours from people who maybe can grind out setting up the meetings instead of them having to do it.*[10]

In other words, having a continual presence on the Hill is just too rich for some groups, or they may not be able to hire long-term lobbyists who have the connections and expertise that they're seeking for the type of advocacy they need to engage in.

Overall, then, relatively poorer groups not only lobby less than relatively richer groups, but relatively richer corporations are also able to have a more continuous lobbying presence through the use of in-house lobbyists—a finding that is visually represented in Figure 7.1. Big corporations and well-funded interest groups can stay ahead of what is happening in Congress. They may not be able to buy specific a legislative outcome, but by anticipating policy in the pipeline they can help shape it in preferred ways. As one lobbyist explained, "You have to play the long game."[11]

Anecdotally, money may also buy a specific *type* of lobbying presence. One lobbyist, himself a revolver (though from bureaucracy) directing a larger advocacy organization, explained that they have a large enough lobbying staff to target who they send to which office: "Well it's a polit-ical town . . . there's very few people that you would characterize as truly independent people. We're all either Republicans or Democrats, and we don't really try and hide that. So, I have Democratic lobbyists and I have Republican lobbyists here."[12] In this case, the lobbyist is describing in-house lobbyists who are obviously politically affiliated and possibly also revolving-door policy advocates. Even so, the same lobbyist also described the circumstances under which he seeks contract help: "The main reason would probably be, you're hiring access. If I'm going to hire an outside lobbyist it's going to be with a purpose."[13] In short, relying on in-house lobbyists does not always mean lower levels of connection or process-expertise, but even when an organization has access to people with consid-erable process expertise, they may *still* need to seek out contract lobbyists on some specific or niche issues. In-house lobbyists may be, on the whole, "cheaper" by the hour than contract lobbyists (LaPira and Thomas 2017), but for the right price, even revolving-door experts can sometimes be con-vinced to join a specific association.

CASE IN POINT: HEALTHY, HUNGER-FREE KIDS AND THEIR VENDING MACHINES

A classic example of watching the pipeline and lobbying for the long game is the alteration of regulations around school vending machines under the

2010 Health, Hunger-Free Kids Act. In writing this law, Congress worked in partnership with Michelle Obama's "Let's Move" campaign to reduce the amount of junk food sold in schools. Major beverage companies, including the Coca-Cola Company and PepsiCo, knew that the regulation was likely to come, and they successfully worked with Congress in crafting the legislation to take full-calorie sodas out of schools but protected vending-machine bottled water and low-calorie sports drink sales in schools. (New USDA rules would remove junk food from school vending machines 2013.) In interviews, a lobbyist discussed the beverage industry's approach to the issue:

We were under attack, admittedly, in a lot of places for selling soft drinks in schools to kids. And being unfairly blamed for the cause, the single cause, of childhood obesity. But, when we really stood back and listened to our consumers, and most importantly, parents, they said to us—"We think, beverage industry, that we should be the decider when it comes to your products. That if our kids, particularly our little kids, are going to drink soft drinks, mom and dad should decide. And when they're in school, we're not there to guide their choices, and it's just sort of free-reign." And it just struck us, schools are special places, and we're parents too. And we decided that it didn't make good public policy sense to anger our consumers. Again, we reject the notion that we are the single cause of obesity. But we try to be responsible. We do that in a lot of ways, calories on the front of pack, etc. We agree to take full-calorie soft drinks out of schools in 2010 and we did. And we did it in conjunction with President Bill Clinton's Alliance for a Healthier Generation. So, we now have basically water, milk, and juice for little kids in elementary and middle schools. In high schools you can have diets, flavored waters if they're not caloric, some sports drinks—but they have to be portion controlled and they're the lower calorie sports drinks. So, you really have a lower calorie, more nutritious, or plain water profile in schools now. So that's governed by the Child Nutrition Act, and we actually worked with Congress to pass that. And the regulations enforcing the new, what they called Smart Snacks Standards in schools just went into effect July 1st. And we worked with USDA and with Congress on that, and we're happy with that.[14]

During policy debates, the industry successfully argued that banning vending machines altogether would result in a loss of revenue for schools.[15] And indeed, schools receive a portion of the vending profits, which they often use to support their extra-curricular programming (Sternberg n.d.). As illustrated by the above narrative, the American Beverage Association (ABA) ultimately supported the legislation and its restrictions because the industry was able to help craft the restrictions in a way that shifted school sales, rather than eliminating them. In an interview with the *New York Times*, ABA Director of Communications Christopher Gindlesperger explained, "Our members have voluntarily reduced the calories in drinks shipped to schools by 88 percent and stopped offering full-calorie soft drinks in school vending machines" (Nixon 2012). In other words, changing the content of vending machines was something the industry had already begun strategizing before the new regulations were proposed. The lobbyist I spoke with touted the Healthy, Hunger Free Kids Act vending regulations as a win for the industry by mitigating potential loss of profits and emerging with an intact reputation for being responsive to parent and consumer preferences.[16]

Both the data and interview anecdotes suggest that for corporations, being wealthier means getting a bigger bang for your [lobbying] buck, so to speak. Wealthier groups hire more long-term lobbyists, and therefore, in the long run, engage in more successful advocacy, particularly because they can still hire contract lobbyists to provide connections and that "kingpin" suave when needed. These groups are able to establish and maintain relationships, monitor important legislative updates, and get ahead of potential policy change when need be. Schattschneider in 1960 critiqued the pluralist "heavenly chorus" for singing with a strong upper-class accent, and that is only becoming truer over time. Political polarization means that legislation takes longer, leadership controls more of the agenda and writes more of the big legislation, and interest groups must keep their ears to the ground to anticipate change or to pursue something through multiple sessions.

This reflects what interest groups report—a higher volume of more persistent lobbying is necessary—it is a long game. And when it comes to how our food is legislated, it is concerning that the ground is slanting more and more in favor of big corporations. Keeping low-calorie beverages in school vending machines certainly helps beverage manufacturers, and it even benefits schools that get to keep some of the profits. Whether the compromise benefits students is for their parents to decide. And yet, while vending machines sell bottled water in the hallways of our nation's high schools, many of these same schools lack drinkable water fountains. Unfortunately, most corporations have little incentive to lobby cities and municipalities to ensure that the water from drinking fountains is clean and delivered through lead-free pipes.

8

Influencing a Polarized Congress

Herculean or Sisyphean?

Congress is responsible for crafting legislation, conducting oversight, and representing the interests of the American public. Yet, increasing pressures such as gridlock, partisan polarization, and the demands of the perpetual campaign have dampened the body's ability to perform these primary functions. Interest groups find themselves working with congressional offices that are under-staffed and whose members are rarely present, and with committees lacking dedicated, non-partisan staff to maintain continuity between leadership changes. Members of Congress are less collegial, less present, and less willing to work across the aisle than ever before. This political polarization and the slow decline of Congress's investment in itself have changed the nature of lobbying.

This book speaks to the ways that interest groups and their lobbyists have adjusted to the changes in Congress and the consequences of those adjustments. As we have seen, individual interest groups have increased their lobbying efforts, a trend with implications for interest group representation and advocacy success. Groups must sustain their lobbying efforts over longer time periods, as Congress debates the same issues session after session. In interviews, lobbyists, and the groups they represent, also reported expanding coalitional work as a tactic for increasing success in the intensely partisan environment of Congress. While it has long been understood that interest groups provide legislative subsidies in the

Farmed Out. Clare R. Brock, Oxford University Press. © Clare R. Brock 2024.
DOI: 10.1093/oso/9780197683798.003.0008

form of information (Hall and Deardorff 2006; Hansen 1991), this book demonstrates that over the last two decades interest groups have moved beyond informational subsidies, and groups now provide Congress with a *negotiation subsidy*, with legislative brokerage and negotiation through the forming of coalitions and provision of political cover in the form of cross-partisan interest group support.

The implications of this finding are worrying from a normative perspective. Much of the day-to-day capacity of the legislature is being underwritten by interest groups and corporations with the deepest pockets, whose priorities may not best represent the majority of Americans. Collectively, we accept lobbying as a part of the political process; we even embrace it as an exercise of free speech and advocacy. Yet, the increasingly lopsided nature of the system, moving further and further toward Schattschneider's proverbial "heavenly chorus" with an upper-class accent, poses a challenge for a representative democracy and consumer society. In the agricultural subsystem, in particular, consumer health, hunger in America, climate policy, the immigration system, and more are all impacted by the decisions made in Congress, and are materially subsidized by interest group lobbying.

The preceding chapters have explored the tactics, strategies, and transformations of corporate and interest group lobbying in the agricultural sector. The legislation written here impacts our health and our wealth by influencing the cost of foods, commodities, and even fuel (in the form of ethanol). Interest groups have always had a weighty hand in determining the outcomes of agricultural policy (Hansen 1991), and yet, the balance may be shifting even more in favor of certain types of groups. Corporations and interest groups, alike, began reporting higher numbers of contacts with legislative offices and hiring more lobbyists over the fifteen years spanned in the analysis. Lobbyists themselves report that, over time, their jobs have become harder, more tense, and require a longer time investment to see success. They also report an increased demand from legislators for interest group coalition-building. Members of Congress prefer to work on issues and legislation that, when possible, has pre-existing cross-cutting support. "Unlikely bedfellows," the proverbial "bootleggers and Baptists"–style partnerships, are a desirable coalitional trait that provides "air cover" to political interests and creates this cross-cutting base of support; given this, interest groups are wise to deliberately seek out such relationships with one another. This strategy is increasingly popular among almost all types of interest groups, and not just in the halls of Congress; such cross-cutting coalitions have also emerged in lobbying bureaucracy (Dwidar 2021).

This book concludes by considering how the increased demands on lobbying groups—both in terms of sustained effort and in the provision of coalitional "air cover"—shape influence and power. Among other things, the findings here confirm what other researchers have found—that "one of the best single predictors of success in the lobbying game is not how much money an organization has on its side, but simply whether it is attempting to protect the policy that is already in place" (Baumgartner et al. 2009, 6). However, in an increasingly acrimonious partisan environment, things have grown worse for those who would seek change—overcoming the status-quo bias of Congress has always been a Herculean task, but for many interest groups the task has become nearly Sisyphean. The stone of the status quo simply keeps rolling back on them. The hyperpartisan environment of Congress is serving to exacerbate the advantage that wealthy groups—especially corporations—enjoy in lobbying. Those groups who can afford sustained advocacy and a steady presence on the Hill and who can afford to hire lobbyists to explicitly specialize in coalition building and management are two steps ahead in the game of influence.

POLARIZATION, PERSISTENCE, AND INFLUENCE

Political scientists once viewed lobbying as a relatively ineffective and weak source of influence on members of Congress (Bauer, Pool, and Dexter 1963). This view has since been discarded, yet scholars still struggle to pinpoint precisely how, when, and why interest groups succeed at influencing Congress. Defenders of the status quo are nearly always at an advantage, but beyond that, interest group influence is still a startlingly elusive phenomenon to pinpoint and measure (Baumgartner et al. 2009). While this book cannot claim to prove the extent of lobbyist influence, it suggests two increasingly important factors in success: persistence and coalition-building.

Chapter 3 built a theory that links the decline in congressional capacity to increased influence from lobbyists. Congress has experienced two simultaneous phenomena that, together, have resulted in a significant decline in congressional capacity. Members of Congress now spend ever greater volumes of effort, time, and resources on the perpetual campaign (Beckel 2017; Klein 2013). Simultaneously, Congress as an institution has decreased the research and staff support it provides for its members. The number of staffers employed in the House, Senate, and by congressional support agencies has steadily declined since the 1980s (Vital Statistics on Congress 2021). Worse, as members spend less time in the office and have fewer support personnel, they also have fewer and weaker relationships with other members of Congress, due in part to partisan polarization. All of this, taken together, ultimately leads to increased congressional gridlock, even as the institution is asked to deal with increasingly complex, technical, and multidimensional policy issues—everything from climate change to cryptocurrency, to social media and technology security issues. As a consequence, Congress has become more prone to passing fewer, higher stakes laws (Brock and Mallinson, forthcoming). Polarization also causes party leaders to keep a tight rein on proposed legislation, often keeping the text of important bills private until the last minute before a vote (Curry 2015). Even within committees, members from the minority party are often excluded from decision-making or viewing proposed legislative text (Curry 2015).

Together, this combination of limited staff, limited time, less collegial relationships, and tighter leadership control over complex policy has resulted in a rank-and-file of Congress that has little access to important information or sufficient time or resources to weigh that information. In response, members increasingly rely on lobbyists to act as "adjunct staffers" to provide policy expertise and research (Boehmke, Gailmard, and Patty 2013; Hall and Deardorff 2006; LaPira and Thomas 2017). In short, lobbyists are more essential than ever.

But these same conditions pose challenges for lobbyists. As members of Congress increasingly suffer from a lack of having the *correct information at the correct time*, lobbyists must sustain their lobbying efforts (and information provision) for longer and increasingly distant time horizons, as the legislative process drags on even minor and seemingly bipartisan issues. The prolonged periods of gridlock force lobbyists to work longer and harder to persevere through a slower process and lobby on an issue from start to finish. In short, in order to impact legislation, interest groups must sustain their lobbying efforts over a longer period of time, often while competing with a greater number of groups also lobbying in the space. The need for persistence means that groups that can afford long-term advocacy strategies over the multiple legislative sessions it now takes to pass most important legislation will be at an inherent advantage. One lobbyist described this as a "soup to nuts" strategy that improved their success: "I think maybe what it is, is doing the soup to nuts—so everything from developing the proposal, writing the legislation, all the way through to seeing it implemented, funded. So, we tend to stick with things, if we pick something we tend to stick with it for a long time."[1] This overall willingness to engage in persistent effort seems to be deeply valuable for advocacy success.

This book has examined the relationship between partisan polarization and increased lobbying effort, looking both at corporate behaviors specifically and at interest groups in the agricultural space more broadly. The evidence suggests that congressional polarization drives lobbying toward Congress, specifically, and that firm revenue is an important influence on the ability to engage in high-volume lobbying (multiple lobbyists, multiple issues, and multiple contacts). Interest groups, corporations, and the lobbyists who advocate on their behalf are engaging in more lobbying, both on an individual level and collectively over time, as a response to the polarized political environment on Capitol Hill. The relationship between polarization and lobbying is essentially self-reinforcing. Lobbying, especially from ideologically oriented think-tank groups, often drives increased polarization (Fagan, McGee, and Thomas 2021); and simultaneously this research demonstrates that political polarization also drives interest groups to lobby harder and longer—it is a two-way causal arrow.

PROVIDING AIR COVER: THE COALITIONAL SUBSIDY AND THE COST OF LOBBYING

Their deteriorating relationships in Congress and the constant campaign force members to demand more from lobbyists than ever before. In response to the extreme partisanship pervading lawmaking in Washington, lobbyists are increasingly turning to coalition-building as both a protection and another form of legislative subsidy to legislators. Cross-cutting coalitions protect lobbying interest groups from pressure to identify too closely with either political party, thereby preserving their options within an increasingly polarized body. Interest groups in the agricultural space, especially corporations, generally reported a preference for remaining non-partisan and building relationships with both Democrats and Republicans. Because food and agriculture legislation is brought up regularly, every five years for the farm bill and in between for other legislation, lobbyists worried about being left "out in the cold" every time party dominance changed hands, if they were perceived as being too closely associated with one party or the other. Additionally, as illustrated, food and agriculture often relies on coalition-building between interests who might naturally tend to skew toward opposite partisan sides or who represent relatively small segments of the voting population. As one lobbyist was quoted talking about coalitions, "When you think U.S. farmers and American farmers, we're probably two percent of the population of that. And so, to advance legislation that is imperative. . . ."[2] By avoiding ideological conflict and partnering with others, these groups mutually increase their chances for success, or at least to avoid being "on the menu."

Chapter 6 used interviews to support the findings from Chapters 3 and 4, providing additional evidence that lobbyists are having to put in more effort over a longer time span in order to feel that they are engaging in effective advocacy. Chapter 6 also explored how lobbyists view working under conditions of extreme partisan polarization. Lobbyists report that the process is longer and more fraught, that they believe that coalition building is almost essential—possibly the only way forward—under these conditions. These findings reaffirm existing evidence that coalition-building is an essential tool for interest group success (Hojnacki 1997; Nelson and Yackee 2012), and they expand on that literature by suggesting that interest groups are actually providing a *benefit to lawmakers* when they engage in coalition-building.

However, interviews with lobbyists also made clear that coalition-building itself is a time-consuming and difficult task. It takes considerable skill and effort to build and maintain a coalition of interest groups and to keep coalition members coordinated and on-message. This means that coalition-building, like lobbying over an extended period of time, may be easier for some groups than for others. In interviews, some lobbyists and groups identified themselves as having particular expertise in coalition-building and maintenance. For contract lobbyists, they often verbalized this as a selling point with their clients. More research is needed to understand the differences between who chooses to specialize in coalition-building and who does not. Nonetheless, this point gets at the interaction of partisan polarization with interest group resources. There is an expanding wealth gap—wealthier business groups have steadily increased their lobbying efforts, while less wealthy businesses have increased at a much slower pace. Wealthier groups are also better able to hire contract lobbyists to engage in continual monitoring and coalition maintenance, as compared to less wealthy businesses, which appear to lobby only intermittently.

It is hardly surprising to argue that wealth appears to have considerable influence over the volume and persistence of interest group lobbying. And yet, historically it has been hard to demonstrate that money leads to more successful lobbying (Baumgartner et al. 2009). As I have argued here, while money may not buy outcomes, it has a more subtle impact—it allows interest groups to exert long-term, sustained influence over legislation that may take several sessions to craft and pass. In *Gaining Access,* Hansen (1991) suggests that direct and frequent interest group access to lawmakers, a function of trust and reputation, is the primary means by which interest groups are able to exert influence. This book demonstrates that, in the current gridlocked climate of continual partisan battling, access is most readily available to groups with the funds to support long-term efforts. Money buys continued presence.

WHAT NEXT?

The statistical analysis in this book ends in 2013, the final year before passage of the Agricultural Act in January 2014. The interviews, while intended to be retrospective, had a more free-flowing nature and often covered strategy and lobbyist thoughts about the political climate as recently as 2018. And yet, politics moves quickly. Where are we now, and what are the implications for policy outcomes?

Pew Center data show that congressional productivity, in terms of substantive laws passed, has steadily declined since the late 1980s (Desilver 2019). Since 2013, we have experienced several more proverbial food fights, often characterized by industry divisions, partisan conflict, and pure crisis. These fights reflect the expanding influence of wealthier interest groups and the implications for interest group advocacy broadly, as well as for agricultural policy specifically. Even as consumers demand more "family farms," "sustainable agriculture," and "organic" products, the kinds of groups that sway Washington, DC, have become less reflective of the spirit of these consumer demands. Additionally, the coalitional marriage between anti-hunger advocates and corporate America leads to questions about pragmatism and defense of the status quo, versus agitation for change. As we will see, lobbying has always favored the rich, powerful, and strong; and it does so now more than ever. In recounting a few of the food battles that have occurred since 2013, these dynamics are clearly in evidence.

INDUSTRY VERSUS CONSUMERS

This book focuses primarily on the impact of partisan battle lines on food lobbying. There are still, of course, those niche issues that cross partisan lines and create new cleavages. Even those relatively bipartisan issues, however, do not escape the consequences of a hyperpartisan political environment.

In 2015, GMO foods[3] stepped into the spotlight when Rep. Mike Pompeo (R-KS) proposed the "Safe and Accurate Food Labeling Act" to block the increasing number of state and local laws from requiring labeling on GMO ingredients and products. Various state and local governments had begun to create a patchwork of different regulatory requirements for product labeling, which on one hand provided the opportunity for "real world tests of policy change" (Harris 2016), but on the other hand created challenges for companies with nationwide distribution changes, now facing wildly different requirements in different localities. Consumer groups deeply opposed the legislation, labeling it the "Deny Consumers the Right to Know, or DARK Act" (Wise 2015). Industry groups like Monsanto, the Biotechnology Industry Organization, and the Grocery Manufacturers Association generally supported Pompeo's legislation and argued that GMOs help feed the world (Lipton 2015). The legislation ultimately passed in the House but died quietly for lack of action in the Senate. In 2016, Congress returned to the topic and passed legislation to require GMO labeling, with a caveat; consumers would be able to see GMO ingredients by scanning a QR Code. No one was pleased with the compromise (Charles 2016). Both the 2015 legislation and the 2016 legislation that eventually passed had bipartisan sponsorship, bipartisan support, and bipartisan opposition. In other words, the battle lines were blurred.

Why was GMO labeling different? There are several possible reasons why GMO labeling has not yet become a partisan issue. One may be that it is generally not a highly salient issue; only 6 percent of the American public say that they closely follow news about GMOs (Pew Research 2016). The majority of Americans hold "soft" views on GMOs and many are not sure how they feel about the topic, regardless of partisanship; Republicans and Democrats, among the public, report virtually identical (lack of) knowledge regarding GMOs (Pew Research 2016). Further, during 2015 and 2016, GMO labeling was highly popular with the public, regardless of partisanship—about two-thirds of Americans supported GMO labeling (Jalonick 2015). Scientists and leaders in the food industry, however, generally were more confident in the safety of GMO foods (Pew Research 2016). And there was strong industry opposition to mandatory labeling laws, particularly from the Grocery Manufacturers Association and certain commodity producers. Unlike SNAP, climate change, and immigration—all issues dealt with in the omnibus farm bill—GMO labeling is not "owned" by one party or the other; rather, the split was public versus private, industry versus consumer. In the end, consumers prevailed, in a weak way. QR codes make the information available, but not easy or convenient to access while strolling down grocery store aisles.

Did partisanship matter when it came to GMO labeling? The short answer is yes. GMO labeling, itself, was not an intensely partisan issue. Its bipartisan support should have made the issue relatively easy, even if industry opposition to labeling resulted in weaker legislation, as ultimately happened. Ultimately, it took two years for Congress to agree on a weak version of GMO labeling that responded to industry concerns but arguably did not reflect consumer interests whatsoever. Congressional gridlock, as a result of partisanship, slows down legislation even when the legislation enjoys bipartisan support. As the legislative process slows, interest groups that are able to afford a sustained presence on the Hill have more opportunity to meet with and discuss issues with members of Congress or their staff. One group discussed their strategy of pursuing issues over long periods of time, saying, "We tend to stick with things for a long period of times. We'll add things, and if something has completely run its course, we'll drop it. But we stick with it, and we do everything," and this sustained presence has had reputational benefits for that group, "though one thing that is true about DC is that, while there's thousands of interest groups and obviously lots of policymakers, so in some ways it's a huge apparatus. In other ways it's kind of a small town. Like the [agriculture] community, everybody doesn't know everybody. But everybody knows people who

[know] everybody else."[4] In other words, lobbyists cultivate and protect their reputations, sometimes over the course of decades in the profession.

One reason behind the increasing value of pursuing matters over long periods of time is the type of advocacy that is becoming more common among successful interest groups—specifically, coalition-building and maintenance. In 2018, years after the GMO labeling law, a lobbyist was discussing a different labeling issue they hoped Congress would tackle:

> *I've got one bill that I'm trying to get introduced for one segment of our industry, regarding labeling, and I want it to be a not very exciting bill with bipartisan support. So I'm working with member companies that have relationships with outside groups. . . to try and build a coalition to move this bill before the end of the year. And it's just time-consuming. None of this happens quickly, especially in this environment where it's highly partisan.*[5]

Coalition building, maintenance, and sustainment is time-consuming, expensive, and challenging. But it is also often a requirement for interest groups or companies who are hoping to see legislation passed, or even who hope to defend their place in the status quo. Notably, the above lobbyist also specifically wished for a "not very exciting" bill that would gain bipartisan support. For groups who are hoping to see change, rather than status quo, the less attention potential legislation attracts, potentially the better, because they're likely to experience less counter-mobilization on the issue (Schattschneider 1960). High-salience issues can also quickly become opportunities for partisan showboating.

Coalitions often have their costs, though. As discussed, some of the most effective coalitions are those comprised of "unlikely bedfellows" or "unholy alliances." Beyond the difficulties of building and maintaining coalitions, these pragmatic alliances can result in sacrificing principles and broader goals. In *Big Hunger*, Andrew Fisher illustrates how the relationship between anti-hunger advocates and corporate partners has often prevented the anti-hunger community from joining campaigns that would address economic inequality more broadly (Fisher 2017, 212). However, these coalitional partnerships have also arguably protected SNAP from some of the most aggressive partisan attacks, as the case of the 2018 farm bill illustrates.

PARTISAN BATTLE LINES AND THE STATUS QUO

The 2018 farm bill, the Agriculture Improvement Act of 2018, might, by final passage numbers, appear less bitterly partisan than the 2014 reauthorization. In fact, its timely completion marked the "first time in nearly 30 years that a farm bill was enacted in the same year in which the programs were authorized" (Newton 2018, n.p.). What's more, the final legislation passed with broadly bipartisan support in both the House and the Senate. By those measures, the bill was a relative success. Partisanship clearly does not mean that nothing gets done. Even so, the process was every bit as partisan and fraught as it was during the 2014 farm bill. As before, the first House Agriculture Committee version of the 2018 bill failed on the House floor, this time not just over SNAP-related disagreements but also because of conflicts over immigration. The SNAP fight was nearly identical; Democrats opposed provisions that would amount to $20 billion in SNAP cuts and impact more than one million people, while some Republicans thought that the cuts weren't deep enough (Golshan 2018). But the new twist came when Republican lawmakers unsuccessfully attempted to use the farm bill as leverage to take action on immigration. House Freedom Caucus members voted against the legislation in retaliation for the perceived overspending in the bill and the lack of a guaranteed future vote on immigration. The vote fell closely along party lines, with all Democrats and thirty Republicans (largely Freedom Caucus members) voting against the bill (Snell and Naylor 2018).

Yet, despite the ideological conflicts between members, relatively little of substance changed in the 2018 farm bill, perhaps explaining its ultimate bipartisan passage. Indeed, despite the nearly constant attacks on SNAP from the early 2000s to present, only limited cuts have occurred, many of which were reversed during the pandemic. Some have argued that the anti-hunger community's tendency to put all their eggs in the SNAP basket makes them potentially vulnerable to attack (Fisher 2017, 212), and yet, such attacks have not yet been successful in a meaningful way.

In the lead-up to the 2018 legislation, then–House Agriculture Committee chair Michael Conaway (R-TX) promised reforms to SNAP, including "to make a rural-urban coalition that is not anchored in food stamps" (Bosso 2017, 167). Nonetheless, the farm and SNAP connection has remained strong, suggesting that the lobbying efforts of anti-hunger groups and their corporate partners, and the ties between agriculture and nutrition programs, are less fragile because of their cross-cutting nature. In *Framing the Farm Bill*, Bosso articulates the relationship well when he says, "Like two partners in an awkward marriage of convenience, never really in love, farm programs and food stamps still need each other, possibly forever" (2017, 168). In short, for anti-hunger advocates, an enormous amount of effort, coalition building, and political capital have gone into maintaining the status quo. But perhaps maintenance, in the face of possible deep cuts, is still a desirable outcome for SNAP recipients and their champions.

CRISIS

While this book focuses on the impact of polarization on lobbying, everything is upended in moments of true national crisis. It is during these moments that the status quo is often shifted. How do crisis, partisanship, and lobbying interact? Coronavirus responses demonstrated that crisis may offer yet another opportunity for lobbyists and the corporations they work for to sway bureaucrats and extract rents from government, but that at the same time, as the proverbial pie is expanded, traditionally disadvantaged groups may also receive benefits.

The COVID-19 pandemic was a major moment in the United States and globally. It was devastating for farm workers, meatpacking workers, and other agricultural laborers across industries. Agriculture, as an industry, suffered enormously. In response, the USDA authorized a multi-billion-dollar assistance package for farms under the auspices of the Coronavirus Aid, Relief, and Economic Security (CARES) Act and the Families First Coronavirus Response (FFCRA) Act ("USDA Announces Coronavirus Food Assistance Program" 2020). More than 170 interest groups and companies lobbied the agency and their members of Congress hoping to influence the distribution of funds (Ramgopal 2020).

The package was billed by Secretary of Agriculture Sonny Perdue as relief that would be offered to farmers "of all sizes and all . . . production" (Ramgopal and Lehren 2020). Instead, the top 1 percent of recipients got more than 20 percent of the money ($1.2 billion); the top 10 percent got over 60 percent; and the bottom 10 percent of recipients got just 0.26 percent (Ramgopal and Lehren 2020). Payments were capped at $250,000 per single farm, but the potential payments were essentially uncapped to those farms structured as "general partnerships." In other words, the biggest and wealthiest businesses in the farming world were able to get far more relief. One hog farming operation received over $6.6 million in pandemic aid; Driscoll Brothers, another commodity producer, received around $4 million; and nearly 870 operations received at least $1 million (Brasher, Nuelle, and Wicks 2021). What's more, just three commodities—cattle, dairy, and corn—got over 80 percent of the money allocated by Congress ("Coronavirus Food Assistance Program 2 Data" 2020). Ultimately, there was little accountability or seeming order for the distribution of funds. Because Congress allowed such broad authority under the CARES and FFCRA Acts, the USDA was able to distribute funds as it saw fit with little transparency. One budget watchdog group called the situation essentially a "shadow farm bill" (Ramgopal 2019).

At the same time, the CARES Act also gave the Agriculture Department broad authority to make it easier for families to apply for and qualify for SNAP, and the Families First Act suspended SNAP's three-month time limit on receiving benefits for certain recipients ("States Are Using Much-Needed Temporary Flexibility in SNAP to Respond to COVID-19 Challenges" 2022). The CARES Act was ultimately passed with overwhelming bipartisan support from Congress, with the support of 90 percent of lawmakers in both houses (Davis, Grisales, and Snell 2020).

Subsequently, the American Recue Plan, passed in 2021, contained an additional $10.4 billion to support agriculture, half of which was earmarked for disadvantaged farmers, debt relief, grants, training, and education, as well as land acquisition assistance (Reiley 2021). However, unlike the CARES Act, the American Rescue Plan was not as overwhelmingly bipartisan. Senate Republicans opposed relief for farmers of color, specifically. Patrick J. Toomey (R-PA), who released a statement saying, "This bill is not about responding to COVID. It is about exploiting the final stretch of a public health crisis in order to enact a longstanding liberal wish-list for years into the future [including] sending payments to farmers and ranchers equal to 120 percent of their borrowings, irrespective of their earnings, wealth or effects from COVID, and exclusively for ethnic minorities or immigrants" (Reiley 2021). The American Rescue Plan contained a wide array of other spending and legislative provisions, including assistance for businesses and for education, and the child tax credit. Ultimately, not a single Republican voted in favor of the bill (Sprunt 2021).

Evidence suggests that crises can, and do, spur congressional action and policy change (Baumgartner and Jones 1993). Additionally, these moments can create rally 'round the flag effects, as we observed in the aftermath of 9/11/2001, which enable presidents to pass their agendas with relatively more ease. However, such moments also create the opportunity for interest groups and corporations to lobby their way into particularized benefits (Alexander, Mazza, and Scholz 2009).

This raises the question, if Congress had possessed a more robust braintrust of experienced researchers, legislative staffers, and nonpartisan support staff, would the outcomes of these omnibus packages have been different? Even more hypothetically, what if Congress were to pass multiple, smaller, and more targeted pieces of legislation? From the 1940s until 2018, Congress increasingly relied on omnibus legislation to accomplish its goals and to encourage party-line voting (Krutz 2001), and since then has relied more on budget reconciliation and appropriations (Krutz 2001). If it had passed specific legislation to address the Covid-related farm crisis, or at least built in more accountability for distribution of funds, instead of allowing the USDA nearly unilateral authority under the CARES Act, for example, would the outcome have been fairer? On the other hand, perhaps without omnibus packaging, SNAP expansion and assistance to marginalized farmers would have been impossible. There is, of course, no way to answer these questions. But asking them provides the opportunity to speculate on how omnibus legislating may offer both opportunities and challenges to effective policymaking, and how the process generates opportunities for particularized benefits that may or may not be to the public's advantage.

CONCLUSIONS

The findings in these chapters suggest some potential areas for future research. While I find that interest groups report an increased reliance on coalition-building as a form of legislative subsidy, more work is needed on how coalition-building functions as a response of political polarization. Which interest groups are most successful at building and maintaining coalitions, and how has that changed in recent years? Interviews with lobbyists frequently noted the challenges of forming and maintaining these cross-partisan coalitions. They also clearly reported that they engage in this kind of behavior more commonly. Yet, this raises additional questions. We need a systematic study on how interest group characteristics are related to successful coalitional work, particularly in these cross-partisan efforts that include "unholy alliances."

This book has also begun to theoretically flesh out a relationship between partisan polarization and longer periods of stasis in the traditional model of punctuated equilibrium. While this appears to be true, makes theoretical sense, and clearly builds from existing research on gridlock (see Binder 1999), additional research is needed to precisely measure the extent to which periods of stasis are increasingly prolonged, and to explore the policy implications of this change in the legislative timeline.

Finally, evidence suggests that partisan polarization is driven by certain types of lobbying (Fagan 2020; Garlick 2021; Gray et al. 2015); this book adds to that literature by showing that polarization also drives lobbying, Together, this evidence indicates a positive reinforcement cycle between partisan polarization and interest group activity. More research is needed to explore the nature of this positive reinforcement dynamic and the speed at which it occurs. Does the substantive policy area matter in the formation of such a cycle?

The evidence presented in this book demonstrates that partisan conflict has forced interest groups to expend greater effort and resources lobbying Congress. Interest groups now not only provide information on the potential impacts and popularity of legislation; groups also provide political air cover and ready-made coalitions in hopes of easing the path for positive action. The increased demands from legislators on interest groups potentially provide more access for interest groups who wish to influence legislative outcomes, but it also means that there is an increasing skew toward better funded organizations who can afford to sustain efforts over multiple congressional sessions, as legislative action drags. In short, a longer and more contentious legislative process exacerbates the already unequal nature of the political system, even as Congress is outsourcing much of its research labor to lobbyists, rather than to personal or committee staffers who have left Congress in droves.

There is a normative cost to the way that partisan polarization has altered the lobbying landscape. Legislators spend more time fighting, flying home, and rallying their bases, and less time on policymaking. Congress has lost expertise and has outsourced brainpower to lobbyists. As lobbying increasingly becomes more skewed toward the ultra-wealthy interest groups and corporations, we risk moving the food system even further from the ideal points of the public. However, these trends can be reversed. Nancy Pelosi recently announced that key House staffers would now be able to earn higher incomes than House members, an effort explicitly aimed toward keeping senior staff, the "institutional brain trust," for longer (Caygle 2021). Slowing the pace of the revolving door is an important step forward in undoing some of the damage that has been done to our legislative branch. Other research offers valuable suggestions for diminishing the partisan divide among the electorate (Mason 2018), a step that one hopes may eventually translate to a more civil, more functional, and more representative Congress.

APPENDIX A

Notes on the Quantitative Methods

Each chapter provides some details about the methods and regressions used within the chapter and makes clear to the reader what dependent variable is being assessed. However, this appendix is provided to clarify additional details, justify the quantitative choices made in analyzing the data, and explain variables with more depth than can be done in the regular flow of main text.

THE DATA

This book relies on an original dataset of lobbying reports to explain how lobbyists are responding to polarization in the food and agriculture policy arena. The original Lobbying Disclosure Act (LDA) of 1995 required lobbying reports from any organization spending or earning more than $10,000 in a six-month period on lobbying the federal government; the legislation has since been updated to cover organizations that spend more than $3,000 on lobbying activities during a given quarter (Office of the Clerk 2021). While these disclosure reports are limited in what they contain, they provide useful, quantifiable measures on lobbying activity, including the issue area interests lobbied in, the number of lobbyists they hired, the institution the lobbyists targeted, and the total amount of money an organization spent on lobbying efforts in a given quarter. However, the data are also "nested and duplicative," meaning that lobbying issue area and lobbying expenditure (for example) cannot be used simultaneously

(LaPira and Thomas, 2020). The Center for Responsive Politics (CRP) has compiled and cleaned all registered lobbying expenditures that have been disclosed through the LDA. This cleaning includes name disambiguation and excludes legal and other non-lobbying expenditures. A full look at the challenges of this data can be found in LaPira and Thomas's paper on LDA analysis (2020).

All statistical analysis contained in this book begins with the year 1998 and extends through the year 2013. This time frame begins when LDA data first became available and extends through the construction of the 2014 farm bill. Interviews are particularly useful for understanding the *why* behind the data analysis presented here. One reason is that LDA data are limited in their scope and are often challenging to parse effectively. An example of the complex nature of the data is that, prior to 2008, lobbying interests were required to report semi-annually, rather than quarterly, meaning that the number of reports of lobbying (the dependent variable in this analysis) doubles in 2008. That is, a lobbyist working for an interest group in 2000 would file two reports a year, while under the new rules beginning in 2008, that same lobbyist began filing four reports a year. To account for the sudden doubling of lobbying reports, a dummy variable was created for the law change in 2007 and was in effect beginning in 2008.[1] This book thus relies on a cross-sectional time-series dataset of lobbying groups from 1998 to 2013.

The analysis in Chapters 4 and 7 relies on a subset of the larger dataset—specifically, it relies on a hand-matched set of corporations that reported lobbying on agricultural issues. I matched the broader set of lobbying interest groups to a dataset downloaded from the WRDS Compustat North America (via Wharton) database that allowed me to identify publicly traded firms reporting lobbying in the larger dataset. The Compustat dataset includes historical descriptive information (headquarter location and revenue, among other things) on stocks from both active and inactive companies from the NYSE, NYSE MKT, NASDAQ, and Arca exchanges.[2] Because firms were named inconsistently in the lobbying data (a function of how firms fill out their reporting forms), I hand-matched the two datasets, resulting in a combined data set including 277 unique, publicly

NOTES ON THE QUANTITATIVE METHODS

traded firms that reported lobbying in the agriculture sector over the sixteen-year time period.

The dependent variable in the analysis throughout much of the book is described as "reports" of lobbying, by institution.[3] Report counts are aggregated by firm, each year. As previously noted, a firm may file a single report each quarter, or it may file multiple reports in a quarter if it employed multiple lobbyists, worked on multiple issue areas, or lobbied in multiple venues.

In the Chapter 4 and Chapter 7 analysis of corporations, this yields 980 observations. However, firms enter and exit the dataset with high frequency, as most firms do not lobby on a consistent basis. Additionally, some firms that lobby regularly choose to report yearly, whether or not they actually lobbied in that issue area, while other firms choose not to. To correct for these variations in firm reporting, I fill in the dataset with zeros for those firms that are present lobbying in the dataset but did not lobby in a particular year. In other words, a firm may report three lobbyists advocating on farm issues in 2002, and zero in 2003. In the data as originally structured, a firm would simply not be present in the data during 2003. However, I have added the firm into the dataset during that year with a zero as their reported number of lobbyists working on agricultural issues. Adding these zeroes increases the total number of observations from 940 to 4,992 corporate lobbying observations.[4]

Between 1998 and 2013, lobbying reports increased steadily, across all institutions. Figure 4.1, found in Chapter 4, illustrates the number of reports made by firms during that time span, by institution. It is important to note that the number of reports filed (the dependent variable) nearly doubles in 2008, after new reporting requirements went into effect. As previously mentioned, I control for this change in reporting requirements in the regression analysis throughout the book.

Simultaneously, while the volume of lobbying done by individual firms was steadily increasing, so was the number of firms engaged in lobbying in the agricultural space (see Figure 3.2). There are noticeable spikes in the number of firms engaging in advocacy during those years when Congress was considering a farm bill.

Chapters 4 and 5 rely on the broader dataset, which includes all interest groups that reported lobbying between 1998 and 2013. There are a total of 2,817 interest groups that reported lobbying in agriculture during this sixteen-year time period, and the unit of analysis is interest group by year, yielding a total of 45,072 observations.[5]

DEPENDENT VARIABLE AND METHODS

In order to test the hypothesis that polarization increases the quantity of lobbying directed toward Congress in Chapters 3 and 4, I perform a negative binomial regression on the cross-sectional, time-series data described here. The dependent variable for each regression, respectively, is the number of lobbyists a firm reported hiring to lobby Congress, the bureaucracy, or the White House in a given year.[6] Lobbying the White House includes those groups that reported lobbying "White House," "Joint Chiefs of Staff," and "Vice President's Office." A group has lobbied Congress if it reports lobbying either the "US Senate" or the "US House of Representatives." Finally, lobbying the bureaucracy is considered lobbying of any other federal unit, ranging from the Department of Commerce and the Office of US Trade Representation to the Department of Agriculture and the Food and Drug Administration, and everything in between.[7] No departments, agencies, or offices were excluded. As noted above, while it would be ideal to measure money spent lobbying these institutions, the way that lobbying disclosure reports are structured does not allow for the possibility of distinguishing how much money was spent on lobbying a particular issue area. Therefore, the number of lobbyists hired in a particular issue area is the best proxy measure for the relative intensity with which a group is engaging in lobbying at any given time.

Analysis of this cross-sectional, time-series dataset in these chapters relies on count data for the dependent variables (see previous paragraph). One important characteristic of lobbying behavior, indicated by the over-dispersion of the data, is that most groups lobby somewhat inconsistently, and they often lobby relatively little when they do report lobbying.

NOTES ON THE QUANTITATIVE METHODS

This means that the data distribution on all of the dependent variables (number of lobbyists, by firm-year) is non-normal and skewed. While time-series analysis approaches can control for serial-dependence in the data, they do not appropriately cope with non-normally distributed data. I have chosen to address the over dispersion of the dataset, rather than the serial dependence problem. A Harris–Tzavalis test provides overwhelming evidence against the presence of a unit root in any of the dependent variables (Lobbying Congress, Lobbying the White House, or Lobbying the Bureaucracy), making autocorrelation less of a concern than overdispersion. A Pearson goodness-of-fit test indicates that the data are too over-disbursed for a Poisson regression, making a time-series negative binomial regression appropriate. I also performed an examination of the variance inflation factors and did not find multi-collinearity between variables.

INDEPENDENT VARIABLES

The independent variables in much of the analysis in this book are as follows. First, I include a dummy variable for those years in which a farm bill is considered by Congress. This accounts for the cyclical nature of decision-making in the agricultural policy space, a characteristic of farm bill re-authorization. It is important to account for this periodicity given that during these years, more groups are likely to lobby, and lobbying groups are likely to lobby more intensely. Similarly, the variable entitled "number of agricultural hearings" (ranging from 10 to 69) is an additional measure of agenda crowding, accounting for other occasional large pieces of legislation that may attract a sudden influx of advocacy as well as the possibility that some farm bill years are more contentious than others.

An additional measure of agenda crowding is the number of other groups lobbying each year, ranging from 31 to 104 groups. Inclusion of the number of groups lobbying each year accounts for the possibility that as more firms begin to lobby, each individual firm will increase its advocacy efforts, lobbying more vociferously due to competition.

The next independent variable, congressional polarization, is a key explanatory variable and is measured as an average of Rosenthal and Poole's House and Senate polarization means on the first dimension, downloaded from Voteview.com.[8] Partisan polarization quantifies the ideological distance between the most far-left and the most far-right members in each chamber.

The measures of divided Congress and unified government are both dummy variables accounting for partisan control over government. Divided partisan control over Congress, in which the House and Senate are controlled by different parties, and unified government, in which Congress and the executive are controlled by the same party, are only correlated about 50 percent of the time.

Finally, in each regression, I include the interest group reports of lobbying in the other two institutions as independent variables. Lobbying in one institution is a strong predictor of lobbying behavior in another institution, because the interest group has already overcome the start-up costs of engaging in advocacy, and because lobbyists are incentivized to create additional markets for themselves (Drutman 2015).

The next set of independent variables, found in Chapters 3 and 6 specifically, account for variation across firms. Only a limited set of firms— generally those with higher revenue—choose to go beyond what can be accomplished through trade associations (Lux, Crook, and Woehr 2011; Mathur and Singh 2011). For this reason, the relative ability of an organization to expend resources on lobbying independently of trade organization (or organizational capacity) is captured by revenue, as reported in Compustat. In the firm-specific dataset, the mean firm revenue is just $21,500, but the maximum firm revenue is $433,500. The majority of firms in this dataset fall well below the mean. Firms below the mean include Kellogg, Hershey's, Horizon Organics, and Land O'Lakes. Firms above the mean include Coca-Cola, Tyson, McDonalds, and Walmart. ConAgra is an example of a firm that falls above the mean some years and falls below it in others. To account for this extreme variation, I normalize firm revenue by taking the log.

NOTES ON THE QUANTITATIVE METHODS

Additionally, the firm dataset connects corporate lobbying efforts with their corporate headquarters location. Within Congress, lobbyists generally target issue-relevant committees, rather than initiating broad, institution-wide efforts (de Figueiredo and Richter 2013; Hojnacki and Kimball 1998, 1999). Following from this, evidence suggests that when groups enjoy strong constituent ties to a legislator's district they will pursue lobbying, regardless of legislator position (Hojnacki and Kimball 1999). Therefore, I include an independent variable capturing the number of representatives on relevant committees that a firm can claim to be a constituent of, based on the location of a firm's headquarters (retrieved from Compustat).[9] I consider "relevant committees" to be the Agriculture Committee, the Appropriations Committee, the Budget Committee, and party leadership. While these are not the *only* committees that have influence over the agricultural policy area, they are arguably the most influential. I also include a second model with an interaction term between firm revenue and firm location (congressional connections measure).[10] As discussed in Chapter 4, while increased resources provide firms with the capacity to lobby outside of trade associations, on their own behalf, and makes them more likely to do so (Lux, Crook, and Woehr 2011; Mathur and Singh 2011), lobbying organizations (of all kinds) also benefit enormously from the ability to make a constituency-based argument to legislators (de Figueiredo and Richter 2013; Hojnacki and Kimball 1998). The interaction term is intended to capture this phenomenon by accounting for the possibility that firms that are *both* wealthy and particularly well connected may have more influence or power than other firms.

APPENDIX B

Notes on Qualitative Methods

ELITE INTERVIEWS

I conducted elite interviews with lobbyists, congressional staffers, and reporters. These interviews were conducted over a series of three research trips to Washington, DC. The first trip occurred during the fall of 2013, the second during the summer of 2014, and the final trip occurred during the spring of 2018.

Readers may notice that, while a few interviewees are named specifically, most have been anonymized in the main text. This reflects several considerations as well as a changing political climate. In general, early interviewees were relatively willing to allow their names to be associated with their words, though many asked to approve quotes if their names were used. By 2018, almost all interviewees requested anonymity. Because of the variety of requests to approve quotes in association with names, others who wanted to control the way that their employer or company was referred to, and so on, I found that it made the most sense to anonymize the vast majority of the quotes.

The Interviewees

Over the course of these interviews, I spoke with twenty-four individuals who work, in some form, with agricultural policy. I spoke with twenty lobbyists from a variety of interest groups, trade associations, and corporations, two reporters, and two legislative staffers. Interviewees were offered anonymity and were encouraged to speak freely about their experiences and opinions.

Obtaining Interviews

The first set of potential interviewees were randomly selected from the Lobbying Disclosure Act data that were used for the quantitative portion of the research. Once a sample of potential interviewees was selected, I contacted the individuals requesting a meeting. While these cold calls resulted in few meetings, it provided a sufficient start. At the end of each interview, I asked for suggestions of important, influential, or interesting individuals who I might contact next; subsequently, all interviews were conducted via snowball sample.

Interview Process

The interviews were in-depth and semi-structured, with primarily open-ended questions guiding the conversations. I allowed interviewees to guide the conversation when possible so that I could discover unanticipated information. I reverted back to prepared questions at intervals when the conversation lagged, with the goal that all interviewees would address the same basic themes and topics.

Every interview began with a brief explanation of the project, a disclosure of all risks, and steps taken to ensure confidentiality. I then asked interviewees for their permission to record our conversation, which I proceeded to do when permission was granted. Interviews for lobbyists, which were my primary targets for this project, tended to run longer and be more in-depth. Lobbyists often spent considerable time explaining challenges specific to their industry or interest and explaining how they interacted with the legislative process to address these challenges. We

NOTES ON QUALITATIVE METHODS

also discussed, at length, their perceptions of how partisanship and political environment have created change in their industry. Interviews with reporters and congressional staffers tended to require a different approach and therefore reveal different information. The study benefited from including perspectives of these other elites, but they were not the primary target or focus of the work.

Sample Questions for Lobbyists

Could you tell me a bit about how you ended up in the position you're in today?

Can you describe an average day to me? What do you think is the most important thing you personally do on a day-to-day basis?

What is an issue you've personally worked on recently?

When you have a new issue, like the one you just mentioned, how do you choose whom to approach or what to do? How do you begin?

Please describe how the political environment for lobbyists has changed over the last ten years.

There's a lot in the news recently about polarization and partisanship. What's your professional experience with that?

Given the partisanship we've been talking about, how does working on an omnibus bill differ from working on a less publicized and more specific issue?

Do you work in coalition groups frequently? Why?

If so, are there particular types of coalitions that you find more effective or less effective?

Is there anything that you do, or that your organization does, that you think is distinct from other lobbying groups?

Is there anything that makes you particularly successful?

Is there anything that I didn't ask you that I should have? Anything I missed?

Is there anyone you know who you think I should talk to, or who might be willing to be interviewed?

May I contact you again if I have any follow-up questions or need clarification on anything?

Do you have any questions for me?

Transcription and Interpretation

Interviews were recorded, allowing me to take notes by hand regarding particularly important information to return to later. Later, I transcribed the 2013 and 2014 interviews by hand and used an automated transcription service to transcribe the 2018 interviews. My method for analyzing transcribed interviews relied on grouping responses together based on question and theme. The goal was to paint a broad picture of how lobbyists perceive the political climate and identify any shifts in their perceptions about their role in crafting policy.

NOTES

CHAPTER 1

1. Author interview with a lobbyist, Washington, DC, July 2015.

CHAPTER 3

1. Author interview with a lobbyist, Washington, DC, March 2018.
2. Author interview with a lobbyist, Washington, DC, March 2014.
3. These alliances are explored more in Chapter 6.
4. Author interview with a lobbyist, Washington, DC, March 2018.
5. In an eerie moment of déjà vu, during the 2020 pandemic recession, the federal government offered to help hog farmers euthanize and dispose of their animals after slowdowns at meatpacking plants left farmers unable to sell their animals (Held 2020).
6. Author interview with a lobbyist, Washington, DC, March 2018.
7. Author interview, Washington, DC, August 2014.
8. Author interview, Washington, DC, August 2014.
9. Author interview with a legislative staffer, Washington, DC, March 2018.
10. Author interview with a lobbyist, Washington, DC, March 2018.
11. Author interview with a lobbyist, Washington, DC, March 2018.
12. Author interview with a lobbyist, Washington, DC, March 2018.
13. Author interview with a lobbyist, Washington, DC, March 2018.
14. Author interview with a lobbyist, Washington, DC, March 2018.
15. Author interview with a legislative staffer, Washington, DC, March 2018.
16. Also known as revolving-door lobbyists; see C3P29.

CHAPTER 4

1. Author interview with Chuck Conner, National Council of Farmer Cooperatives, Washington, DC, August 2014.

2. Portions of this chapter were first published in "Partisan Polarization and Corporate Lobbying: Information, Demand, and Conflict," *Interest Groups and Advocacy*, 10, no. 2 (2021): 95–113. https://dio.org/10.1057/s41309-021-00112-5.
3. Author interview with a lobbyist, Washington, DC, March 2018.
4. Complete descriptions can be found in Appendix A.
5. Author interview with a lobbyist, Washington, DC, April 2014.
6. Author interview with a lobbyist, Washington, DC, April 2014.
7. Author interview with a lobbyist, Washington, DC, April 2014.
8. Author interview with a lobbyist, Washington, DC, March 2018.

CHAPTER 5

1. It is worth noting that farm bill vetoes have been incredibly rare, with a previous farm bill veto occurring under President Dwight D. Eisenhower (see Eisenhower 1956).
2. Described completely in Appendix A.
3. Author interview with a lobbyist, Washington, DC, March 2018.
4. A Pearson goodness-of-fit test indicates that the data are too over-disbursed for a poisson regression, making a time-series negative binomial regression appropriate. I also performed an examination of the variance inflation factors and did not find multicoliniarity between variables.
5. As described in Chapter 4 for the lobbying firms, the data distribution in this chapter on all of the dependent variables (number of lobbyists, by interest group–year) is non-normal and skewed. While time-series analysis approaches can control for serial-dependence in the data, they do not appropriately cope with non-normally distributed data. I have chosen to address the overdispersion of the dataset, rather than the serial dependence problem. A Harris–Tzavalis test provides overwhelming evidence against the presence of a unit root in any of the dependent variables (Lobbying Congress, Lobbying the White House, or Lobbying the Bureaucracy), making autocorrelation less of a concern than overdispersion. A Pearson goodness-of-fit test indicates that the data are too overdispersed for a Poisson regression, making a time-series negative binomial regression appropriate. I also performed an examination of the variance inflation factors and did not find multicollinearity between variables.
6. Author interview with a lobbyist, Washington, DC, April 2014.

CHAPTER 6

1. These twenty-four interviews included individuals from nine trade associations; four congressional staffers; four in-house corporate lobbyists; four contract lobbyists; two journalists; and one formal coalition.
2. A full description of interview methodology and the pre-determined questions can be found in Appendix B.
3. Author interview with a lobbyist, Washington, DC, April 2014.
4. Author interview with a lobbyist, Washington, DC, March 2018.
5. Author interview with a lobbyist, Washington, DC, April 2014.

NOTES 157

6. Author interview with a lobbyist, Washington, DC, April 2014.
7. Literature on lobbying has long recognized that lobbyists look for legislative champions to sponsor their policy preferences in Congress; this is not new. See, for example, *Networks of Champions: Leadership, Access, and Advocacy in the U.S. House of Representatives* (DeGregorio 2010).
8. Author interview with a lobbyist, Washington, DC, March 2018.
9. Author interview with a lobbyist, Washington, DC, March 2018.
10. Author interview with a lobbyist, Washington, DC, March 2018.
11. Author interview with a lobbyist, Washington, DC, March 2018.
12. Author interview with a lobbyist, Washington, DC, March 2018.
13. Author interview with a lobbyist, Washington, DC, March 2018.
14. Author interview with a lobbyist, Washington, DC, March 2018.
15. Author interview with a lobbyist, Washington, DC, March 2018.
16. Author interview with a lobbyist, Washington, DC, April 2014.
17. Author interview with a lobbyist, Washington, DC, April 2014.
18. Author interview with a lobbyist, Washington, DC, March 2018.
19. Author interview with a lobbyist, Washington, DC, March 2018.
20. Author interview with a lobbyist, Washington, DC, March 2018.
21. Author interview with a lobbyist, Washington, DC, March 2018.
22. Author interview with a lobbyist, Washington, DC, March 2018.
23. Author interview with a lobbyist, Washington, DC, March 2018.
24. Author interview with a lobbyist, Washington, DC, March 2018.
25. Author interview with a lobbyist, Washington, DC, March 2018.
26. Author interview with a lobbyist, Washington, DC, March 2018.

CHAPTER 7

1. Author interview with a lobbyist, Washington, DC, March 2018.
2. While it would be ideal to discover whether a resource gap exists among all interest groups or just corporations, revenue and relative resource data are not easily collected from interest groups, writ large.
3. The correlation coefficient is .17 and is significant at the .01 level.
4. Normalizing firm revenue here is visually helpful, since firms reported wildly different revenues over time—from some firms reporting zero revenue to firms reporting a revenue of $500,000 in the same time frame.
5. Some corporations may also choose to hire a contract lobbyist on retainer. While this is an interesting and important strategic choice, it is indistinguishable in the dataset from the decision to hire a contract lobbyist for a specific legislative issue.
6. Author interview with a lobbyist, Washington, DC, April 2014.
7. Author interview with a lobbyist, Washington, DC, April 2014.
8. Due to the nature and restrictions of multinomial logit, I do not consider how many lobbyists a corporation used of each type; using three in-house lobbyists is treated the same as using one. The question under consideration here is the strategy of relying on in-house versus contract lobbyists or relying on both in combination.

9. A full description of the dataset and independent variables can be found in Appendix A.
10. Author interview with a lobbyist, Washington, DC, April 2014.
11. Author interview with a lobbyist, Washington, DC, March 2018.
12. Author interview with a lobbyist, Washington, DC, April 2014.
13. Author interview with a lobbyist, Washington, DC, April 2014.
14. Author interview with a lobbyist, Washington, DC, April 2014.
15. Author interview with a lobbyist, Washington, DC, March 2018.
16. Author interview with a lobbyist, Washington, DC, March 2018.

Chapter 8

1. Author interview with a lobbyist, Washington, DC, April 2014.
2. Author interview with a lobbyist, Washington DC, March 2018.
3. GMO stands for Genetically Modified Organism. One common use of genetic modification is to make a crop more resistant to certain pests or tolerate herbicides. There are relatively few GMO crops produced in the United States, many of which are used for animal feed. The following are the GMO crops grown in the US: corn, soybean, cotton, potato, papaya, summer squash, canola, alfalfa, apple, and sugar beet (GMO Crops, Animal Food, and Beyond 2020).
4. Author interview with a lobbyist, Washington, DC, April 2014.
5. Author interview with a lobbyist, Washington, DC, March 2018.

Appendix A

1. All reports filed before 2008 have a 0, while all reports filed during or after 2008 are designated with a 1. To fully understand the necessity of this dummy variable, it is necessary to thoroughly understand the structure of LDA forms and the data that they produce. See the cited LaPira and Thomas 2020 paper.
2. The COMPUSTAT database "provides more than 300 annual and 100 quarterly Income Statement, Balance Sheet, Statement of Cash Flows, and supplemental data items, on approximately 10,000 actively traded companies and 8,000 inactive companies" (WRDS Compustat Database (via Wharton) n.d.).
3. The actual physical form used to report lobbying, filed by a corporation or interest group, may include multiple lobbyists, issues, and interactions with multiple institutions. However, it is nonetheless useful and descriptive to refer to any specific report of lobbyist-legislature interaction as being a "report," with the understanding that the terminology is not synonymous with the physical form that an interest group fills out.
4. While using a zero-inflated model would be desirable under these conditions, it is not possible to use both a zero-inflated model and control for the time-series element. I have chosen to address the time-series nature of the data, rather than the problem of zero inflation.

NOTES 159

5. Again, as in Chapter 4, interest groups enter and exit the dataset with high frequency, as most groups do not lobby on a consistent basis. Additionally, some groups that lobby regularly choose to report yearly, whether or not they actually lobbied in that issue area, while other firms choose not to. To correct for these variations in firm reporting, the data set is filled in with zeros for those groups that are present lobbying in the dataset but did not lobby in a particular year.

6. Firms fill out lobbying reports four times per year, assuming they meet the minimum requirements. Each report includes an appropriate place to disclose institution lobbied, as well as which lobbyists interacted with that institution. For instance, a report might indicate that contract lobbyist A lobbied the House and the Senate; and in-house lobbyist B lobbied the FDA.

7. Data were not restricted based on which agencies were lobbied. If the lobbying issue reported was categorized as "agriculture," then it was included in the database. An exhaustive list of all agencies found in the data would be quite long. Examples of additional agencies lobbied include the Department of Energy, Department of Homeland Security, Office of US Trade Representation, Department of Commerce, Department of Advanced Research Projects Agency, Department of Interior, Department of Treasury, and many, many others.

8. Including separate measures of polarization in the House and Senate, as opposed to averaging the two, made no appreciable difference in regression results.

9. It would be ideal to use employment at various corporate locations, rather than simply corporate headquarters location, to determine constituency relationships. Unfortunately, collecting this data is highly impractical, if not impossible.

10. The interaction term is the firm revenue (normalized by logging), multiplied times the number of "constituency connections" a firm has to members of Congress on relevant committees.

REFERENCES

CHAPTER 1 CITATIONS

Aubrey, Allison. 2014. "Health Advocates Lament GOP Move to Relax School Lunch Rules." NPR. https://www.npr.org/sections/thesalt/2014/05/30/317161292/health-advocates-lament-gop-move-to-relax-school-lunch-rules (accessed December 15, 2022).

Bauer, Raymond Augustine, Ithiel de Sola Pool, and Lewis Anthony Dexter. 1963. *American Business and Public Policy: The Politics of Foreign Trade.* Atherton: Atherton Press.

Baumgartner, Frank R., and Beth L. Leech. 1998. *Basic Interests: The Importance of Groups in Politics and in Political Science.* Princeton: Princeton University Press.

Bittman, Mark. 2011. "The Secret Farm Bill." *New York Times,* November 8, 2011. https://archive.nytimes.com/opinionator.blogs.nytimes.com/2011/11/08/the-secret-farm-bill/ (accessed December 14, 2022).

Boebert, Lauren. [@laurenboebert]. 2021, April 24. "Lauren Boebert on Twitter: 'Joe Biden's Climate Plan Includes Cutting....'" [Tweet] https://archive.ph/aHJ96 (accessed October 21, 2022).

Bosso, Christopher J. 2017. *Framing the Farm Bill: Interests, Ideology, and Agricultural Act of 2014.* Lawrence: University Press of Kansas.

Confessore, Nicholas. 2014. "How School Lunch Became the Latest Political Battleground." *New York Times,* October 7, 2014. https://www.nytimes.com/2014/10/12/magazine/how-school-lunch-became-the-latest-political-battleground.html (accessed June 17, 2021).

Curry, James. 2015. *Legislating in the Dark.* Chicago: University of Chicago Press.

Drutman, Lee. 2015. *The Business of America Is Lobbying: How Corporations Became Politicized and Politics Became More Corporate.* Oxford: Oxford University Press.

Evich, Helena Bottemiller. 2014. "Behind the School Lunch Fight." *POLITICO,* June 4, 2014. https://www.politico.com/story/2014/06/michelle-obama-public-school-lunch-school-nutrition-association-lets-move-107390 (accessed June 21, 2021).

Fisher, Andrew. 2017. *Big Hunger: The Unholy Alliance between Corporate America and Anti-Hunger Groups*. Cambridge, MA: MIT Press.

"Food Distribution." https://www.usda.gov/topics/food-and-nutrition/food-distribut ion (accessed June 16, 2021).

Hall, Richard L., and Alan V. Deardorff. 2006. "Lobbying as Legislative Subsidy." *American Political Science Review* 100(1): 69–84.

Hansen, John Mark. 1991a. *Gaining Access: Congress and the Farm Lobby, 1919–1981*. Chicago: University of Chicago Press.

"Let's Move: Achievements." *Let's Move!* https://letsmove.obamawhitehouse.archives. gov/achievements (accessed December 15, 2022).

Levine, Susan. 2008. *School Lunch Politics*. Princeton: Princeton University Press.

Lowi, Theodore J. 1969. *The End of Liberalism: The Second Republic of the United States*. 40th anniv. ed. New York: W. W. Norton.

Mason, Lilliana. 2018. *Uncivil Agreement: How Politics Became Our Identity.*. Chicago: University of Chicago Press.

McCarthy, Bill. 2021. "Joe Biden Banning Burgers? Fox News, GOP Politicians Fuel False Narrative." *PolitiFact*, April 26, 2021. https://www.politifact.com/factchecks/ 2021/apr/26/fox-news-channel/joe-biden-banning-burgers-fox-news-gop-politici ans/ (accessed October 21, 2022).

Nixon, Ron. 2013. "Lobbying Heats Up before Farm Talks." *New York Times,* October 23, 2013. https://www.nytimes.com/2013/10/24/us/lobbying-heats-up-ahead-of-farm-bill-talks.html (accessed June 15, 2021).

Overby, Peter. 2014. "Lobbyists Loom behind the Scenes of School Nutrition Fight." NPR, June 11, 2014. https://www.npr.org/sections/thesalt/2014/06/11/320753007/behind-the-scenes-of-school-nutrition-fight-big-food-money-flows (accessed June 17, 2021).

Rogers, David. 2013. "How the Farm Bill Failed." *POLITICO*, June 23, 2013. https://www. politico.com/story/2013/06/how-the-farm-bill-failed-093209 (accessed June 15, 2021).

Schwartz, Colin, and Margo G. Wootan. 2019. "How a Public Health Goal Became a National Law." *Nutrition Today* 54(2): 67–77.

Sesame Street. 2009. *Sesame Street: Michelle Obama and Elmo—Healthy Habits*. https:// www.youtube.com/watch?v=GhGWSfraeyQ (accessed December 15, 2022).

Sheingate, Adam D. 2003. *The Rise of the Agricultural Welfare State: Institutions and Interest Group Power in the United States, France, and Japan*. Princeton: Princeton University Press.

Siegel, Bettina Elias. 2019. *Kid Food: The Challenge of Feeding Children in a Highly Processed World*. Ashland: Blackstone Publishing.

Upton, Cecily, and Dorothy S. McAuliffe. 2019. "Our Hidden Infrastructure Crisis: School Cafeterias." *The Hill,* October 15, 2019. https://thehill.com/opinion/education/ 465872-our-hidden-infrastructure-crisis-school-cafeterias/ (accessed December 6, 2022).

CHAPTER 2 CITATIONS

"A Short History of SNAP." 2018. *USDA Food and Nutrition Service*. https://www.fns. usda.gov/snap/short-history-snap (accessed September 27, 2022).

REFERENCES

Bosso, Christopher J. 2017. *Framing the Farm Bill: Interests, Ideology, and Agricultural Act of 2014*. Lawrence: University Press of Kansas.

Browne, William P. 1988. *Private Interests, Public Policy, and American Agriculture*. Lawrence: University Press of Kansas.

Congressional Record: Proceedings and Debates of the 104th Congress, Second Session. 1996. Washington, DC: Congress. https://www.govinfo.gov/content/pkg/CREC-1996-02-28/pdf/CREC-1996-02-28-house.pdf.

Devarenne, Sidonie, and Bailey DeSimone. "History of the United States Farm Bill." *Library of Congress*. https://www.loc.gov/ghe/cascade/index.html?appid=1821e 70c01de48ae899a7ff708d6ad8b&bookmark=Farm%20Bills (accessed September 26, 2022).

Doering, Otto, and Phil Paarlberg. 1999. *Critical Questions about the Farm Crisis: Causes and Remedies*. Purdue. https://ag.purdue.edu/commercialag/home/paer-article/criti cal-questions-about-the-farm-crisis-causes-and-remedies/ (accessed September 28, 2022).

"Farm Bill Spending." 2022. USDA ERS. https://www.ers.usda.gov/topics/farm-econ omy/farm-commodity-policy/farm-bill-spending/ (accessed September 26, 2022).

Finegold, Kenneth. 1995. *State and Party in America's New Deal*. Madison: University of Wisconsin Press.

Frates, Chris. 2011. "David Obey Heading to K Street." *POLITICO*, June 3, 2011. https:// www.politico.com/story/2011/06/david-obey-heading-to-k-street-056203 (accessed October 29, 2022).

Gais, Thomas L., Mark A. Peterson, and Jack L. Walker. 1984. "Interest Groups, Iron Triangles and Representative Institutions in American National Government." *British Journal of Political Science* 14(2): 161–85.

Gunderson, Gordon W. 2003. *The National School Lunch Program: Background and Development*. Hauppauge: Nova Publishers.

Hansen, John Mark. 1991a. *Gaining Access: Congress and the Farm Lobby, 1919–1981*. Chicago: University of Chicago Press.

Hansen, John Mark. 1991b. *Gaining Access: Congress and the Farm Lobby, 1919-1981*. University of Chicago Press.

Levine, Susan. 2008. *School Lunch Politics*. Princeton:

Nelson, Frederick J, and Lyle P Schertz. 1996. *Provisions of the Federal Agriculture Improvement and Reform Act of 1996*. USDA ERS.

Proceedings of the National Nutrition Conference for Defense: May 26, 27, and 28, 1941, Called by President Franklin D. Roosevelt. 1942. U.S. Government Printing Office.

Risser, James, and George Anthan. 1976. "Why They Love Earl Butz." *New York Times*, June 13, 1976. https://www.nytimes.com/1976/06/13/archives/why-they-love-earl-butz-pro sperous-farmers-see-him-as-the-greatest.html (accessed September 27, 2022).

Schaffer, Harwood D., and Daryll E. Ray. 2018. "Benchmarking Ag Policies." *Agricultural Policy Analysis Center*, June 27, 2018. http://www.agpolicy.org/weekcol/2018/934.html (accessed October 29, 2022).

Sheingate, Adam. 2013. "The Future of Farm Bills." *The Monkey Cage*, June 28, 2013. http://themonkeycage.org/2013/06/the-future-of-farm-bills/ (accessed March 8, 2017).

Sheingate, Adam D. 2003. *The Rise of the Agricultural Welfare State: Institutions and Interest Group Power in the United States, France, and Japan.* Princeton: Princeton University Press.

Theriault, Sean M. 2013. *The Gingrich Senators: The Roots of Partisan Warfare in Congress.* Oxford: Oxford University Press.

Worsham, Jeffrey. 2006. "Up in Smoke: Mapping Subsystem Dynamics in Tobacco Policy." *Policy Studies Journal* 34(3): 437–52.

CHAPTER 3 CITATIONS

"2008: Dole and McGovern: The World Food Prize." World Food Prize Foundation. https://www.worldfoodprize.org/en/laureates/20002009_laureates/2008_dole_and_mcgovern/ (accessed October 21, 2022).

Alexander, Raquel Meyer, Stephen W. Mazza, and Susan Scholz. 2009. *Measuring Rates of Return for Lobbying Expenditures: An Empirical Case Study of Tax Breaks for Multinational Corporations.* Rochester, NY: Social Science Research Network. SSRN Scholarly Paper. http://papers.ssrn.com/abstract=1375082 (accessed November 4, 2013).

Ansolabehere, Stephen, John M. de Figueiredo, and James Snyder. 2003. "Why Is There So Little Money in U.S. Politics." *Journal of Economic Perspectives* 17(1): 105–20.

Bauer, Raymond Augustine, Ithiel de Sola Pool, and Lewis Anthony Dexter. 1963. *American Business and Public Policy: The Politics of Foreign Trade.* Atherton: Atherton Press.

Baumgartner, Frank R., Jeffrey M. Berry, Marie Hojnacki, David C. Kimball, and Beth L. Leech. 2009. *Lobbying and Policy Change: Who Wins, Who Loses, and Why.* Chicago: University of Chicago Press.

Baumgartner, Frank R., and Bryan D. Jones. 1993a. *Agendas and Instability in American Politics.*2nd ed. Chicago: University of Chicago Press.

Baumgartner, Frank R, and Bryan D. Jones . 1993b. *Agendas and Instability in American Politics.* 2nd ed. Chicago: University of Chicago Press.

Baumgartner, Frank R., and Beth L. Leech. 1998. *Basic Interests: The Importance of Groups in Politics and in Political Science.* Princeton.: Princeton University Press.

Baumgartner, Frank R., and Beth L. Leech. 2001. "Interest Niches and Policy Bandwagons: Patterns of Interest Group Involvement in National Politics." *Journal of Politics* 63(04): 1191–1213.

Beckel, Michael. 2017. *The Price of Power: A Deep-Dive Analysis into How Political Parties Squeeze Influential Lawmakers to Boost Campaign Coffers.* Washington, DC: Issue One. https://www.issueone.org/wp-content/uploads/2017/05/price-of-power-final.pdf.

Binder, Sarah A. 1999. "The Dynamics of Legislative Gridlock, 1947-96." *The American Political Science Review* 93(3): 519–33.

Blau, Benjamin M., Tyler Brough, and Diana Weinert Thomas. 2011. *Corporate Lobbying, Political Connections, and the 2008 Troubled Asset Relief Program.* Rochester, NY: Social Science Research Network. SSRN Scholarly Paper. http://papers.ssrn.com/abstract=1878653 (accessed November 4, 2013).

REFERENCES

Boehmke, Frederick J., Sean Gailmard, and John W. Patty. 2013. "Business as Usual: Interest Group Access and Representation across Policy-Making Venues." *Journal of Public Policy* 33(1): 3–33.

Bosso, Christopher J. 2017. *Framing the Farm Bill: Interests, Ideology, and Agricultural Act of 2014.* Lawrence: University Press of Kansas.

Brock, Clare R., and Daniel Mallinson. Forthcoming. "Measuring the Stasis: Punctuated Equilibrium Theory and Partisan Polarization." *Policy Studies Journal.*

Burns, John J. 2012. "Archives Diary: Tip O'Neill and Bipartisan Friendships 'After 6 p.m.'" *John J. Burns Library's Blog,* October 22, 2012. https://johnjburnslibrary. wordpress.com/2012/10/22/archives-diary-tip-oneill-and-bipartisan-friendships-after-6-p-m/ (accessed December 7, 2022).

Campiche, Jody, and Larry D. Sanders. 2017. "Another Farm Bill Expiration: How Did We Get Here, What Does It Mean, and What Happens Now? – Oklahoma State University." *OSU Extension,* March 2017. https://extension.okstate.edu/fact-sheets/another-farm-bill-expiration-how-did-we-get-here-what-does-it-mean-and-what-happens-now.html (accessed June 22, 2020).

Curry, James. 2015. *Legislating in the Dark.* Chicago: University of Chicago Press. https://www.press.uchicago.edu/ucp/books/book/chicago/L/bo20832419.html (accessed October 24, 2018).

de Figueiredo, John M. 2002. "Lobbying and Information in Politics." *Business and Politics* 4(2): 125–29.

Denzau, Arthur T., and Michael C. Munger. 1986. "Legislators and Interest Groups: How Unorganized Interests Get Represented." *The American Political Science Review* 80(1): 89–106.

Draper, Robert. 2022. "The Problem of Marjorie Taylor Greene." *New York Times.* https://www.nytimes.com/2022/10/17/magazine/marjorie-taylor-greene.html (December 7, 2022).

Dwidar, Maraam A. 2021. "Diverse Lobbying Coalitions and Influence in Notice-and-Comment Rulemaking." *Policy Studies Journal* 50(1): 199–240. https://onlinelibrary. wiley.com/doi/abs/10.1111/psj.12431 (accessed July 28, 2021).

Evers-Hillstrom, Karl. 2021. "Most Expensive Ever: 2020 Election Cost $14.4 Billion." *OpenSecrets,* February 11, 2021. https://www.opensecrets.org/news/2021/02/2020-cycle-cost-14p4-billion-doubling-16/ (accessed December 7, 2022).

Good, Keith. 2014. "President Obama Signs 2014 Farm Bill Into Law." *Farm Policy.* http://farmpolicy.com/2014/02/08/weekend-update-president-obama-signs-2014-farm-bill-into-law/ (accessed March 2, 2017).

Grier, Kevin B., and Michael C. Munger. 1993. "Comparing Interest Group PAC Contributions to House and Senate Incumbents, 1980-1986." *Journal of Politics* 55(3): 615–43.

Hall, Richard L., and Alan V. Deardorff. 2006. "Lobbying as Legislative Subsidy." *American Political Science Review* 100(1): 69–84.

Hall, Richard L., and Frank W. Wayman. 1990. "Buying Time: Moneyed Interests and the Mobilization of Bias in Congressional Committees." *American Political Science Review* 84(3): 797–820.

Hansen, John Mark. 1991. *Gaining Access: Congress and the Farm Lobby, 1919–1981*. Chicago: University of Chicago Press.

Held, Lisa. 2020. "Struggling Farmers Are Selling Midwest Hogs Ad Hoc and Online." *Civil Eats*, June 8, 2020. https://civileats.com/2020/06/08/struggling-farmers-are-selling-midwest-hogs-ad-hoc-and-online/ (June 22, 2020).

Hill, Matthew D., G. W. Kelly, G. Brandon Lockhart, and Robert A. Van Ness. 2013. *Determinants and Effects of Corporate Lobbying*. Rochester, NY: Social Science Research Network. SSRN Scholarly Paper. http://papers.ssrn.com/abstract=1420224 (accessed November 4, 2013).

Hochberg, Yael V., Paola Sapienza, and Annette Vissing-Jørgensen. 2009. "A Lobbying Approach to Evaluating the Sarbanes-Oxley Act of 2002." *Journal of Accounting Research* 47(2): 519–83.

Hojnacki, Marie, and David C. Kimball. 1998. "Organized Interests and the Decision of Whom to Lobby in Congress." *American Political Science Review* 92(4): 775–90.

Holmes, Frank. 2022. "Consumer Spending Looks Strong Heading into the Holiday Shopping Season." *Forbes,* November 21, 2022. https://www.forbes.com/sites/greatspeculations/2022/11/21/consumer-spending-looks-strong-heading-into-the-holiday-shopping-season/ (accessed December 7, 2022).

Klein, Ezra. 2013. "The Most Depressing Graphic for Members of Congress." *Washington Post,* January 14, 2013. https://www.washingtonpost.com/news/wonk/wp/2013/01/14/the-most-depressing-graphic-for-members-of-congress/ (accessed March 24, 2021).

Langbein, Laura I. 1993. "PACs, Lobbies and Political Conflict: The Case of Gun Control." *Public Choice* 77(3): 551–72.

LaPira, Timothy M., and Herschel F. Thomas III. 2017. *Revolving Door Lobbying: Public Service, Private Influence, and the Unequal Representation of Interests*. Lawrence: University Press of Kansas.

Levine, Susan. 2008. *School Lunch Politics*. Princeton: Princeton University Press.

Lewis, Jeffrey B., Keith Poole, Howard Rosenthal, Adam Boche, Aaron Rudkin, and Luke Sonnet. 2021. "Voteview: Congressional Roll-Call Votes Database." https://www.voteview.com/articles/party_polarization (accessed February 1, 2021).

Liu, Huchen. 2021. "Campaign Contributions and Access to Congressional Offices: Patterns in Foreign Lobbying Data." *Political Research Quarterly* 75(3): 812–28.

Lorenz, Geoffrey Miles. 2019. "Prioritized Interests: Diverse Lobbying Coalitions and Congressional Committee Agenda Setting." *Journal of Politics* 82(1): 225–40.

Lux, Sean, T. Russell Crook, and David J. Woehr. 2011. "Mixing Business With Politics: A Meta-Analysis of the Antecedents and Outcomes of Corporate Political Activity." *Journal of Management* 37(1): 223–47.

Mason, Lilliana. 2018. *Uncivil Agreement: How Politics Became Our Identity*. Chicago: University of Chicago Press.

Mathur, Ike, and Manohar Singh. 2011. *Corporate Political Strategies*. Rochester, NY: Social Science Research Network. SSRN Scholarly Paper. http://papers.ssrn.com/abstract=1774328 accessed (November 4, 2013).

McKay, Amy. 2019. "Buying Amendments? Lobbyists' Campaign Contributions and Microlegislation in the Creation of the Affordable Care Act." *Legislative Studies Quarterly* 45(2): 327–360.

REFERENCES

Mian, Atif, Amir Sufi, and Francesco Trebbi. 2010. "The Political Economy of the US Mortgage Default Crisis." *American Economic Review* 100(5): 1967–98.

Milyo, Jeffrey, David Primo, and Timothy Groseclose. 2000. "Corporate PAC Campaign Contributions in Perspective." *Business and Politics* 2(1): 75–88.

Nelson, David, and Susan Webb Yackee. 2012. "Lobbying Coalitions and Government Policy Change: An Analysis of Federal Agency Rulemaking." *Journal of Politics* 74(2): 339–53.

Reynolds, Molly. 2021. *Vital Statistics on Congress.* Brookings Institution. https://www.brookings.edu/wp-content/uploads/2019/03/Chpt-5.pdf.

Richter, Brian Kelleher. 2011. *'Good' and 'Evil': The Relationship Between Corporate Social Responsibility and Corporate Political Activity.* Rochester, NY: Social Science Research Network. SSRN Scholarly Paper. http://papers.ssrn.com/abstract=1750368 (accessed November 4, 2013).

Rogers, David. 2013. "How the Farm Bill Failed." *POLITICO,* June 23, 2013. http://politi.co11Ux2zb (accessed October 6, 2016).

Sadowski, Jathan. 2012. "The Much-Needed and Sane Congressional Office That Gingrich Killed Off and We Need Back." *The Atlantic,* October 26, 2012. https://www.theatlantic.com/technology/archive/2012/10/the-much-needed-and-sane-congressional-office-that-gingrich-killed-off-and-we-need-back/264160/ (accessed March 1, 2023).

Schattschneider, E. E. 1957. "Intensity, Visibility, Direction and Scope." *American Political Science Review* 51(4): 933–42.

Sheingate, Adam. 2013. "The Future of Farm Bills." *The Monkey Cage,* June 28, 2013. http://themonkeycage.org/2013/06/the-future-of-farm-bills/ (accessed March 8, 2017).

Sheingate, Adam. 2021. "Why Does the Farm Bill Divide the House Majority?" *3Streams,* January 8, 2021. https://medium.com/3streams/policy-regime-decay-6d69e26fc056 (accessed August 30, 2023).

Stein, Jeff. 2018. "Congress Just Passed an $867 Billion Farm Bill. Here's What's in It." *Washington Post,* December 12, 2018. https://www.washingtonpost.com/business/2018/12/11/congresss-billion-farm-bill-is-out-heres-whats-it/?noredirect=on&utm_term=.3c1fdf2e94b0 (accessed January 6, 2019).

Stratmann, Thomas. 1991. "What Do Campaign Contributions Buy? Deciphering Causal Effects of Money and Votes." *Southern Economic Journal* 57(3): 606–20.

Theriault, Sean M. 2013. *The Gingrich Senators: The Roots of Partisan Warfare in Congress.* Oxford: Oxford University Press.

Vital Statistics on Congress. 2021. Brookings Institution. https://www.brookings.edu/multi-chapter-report/vital-statistics-on-congress/ (accessed March 31, 2021).

Welch, W. P. 1982. "Campaign Contributions and Legislative Voting: Milk Money and Dairy Price Supports." *Western Political Quarterly* 35(4): 478–95.

Wright, John R. 1990. "Contributions, Lobbying, and Committee Voting in the U.S. House of Representatives." *American Political Science Review* 84(2): 417–38.

Yu, Frank, and Xiaoyun Yu. 2012. "Corporate Lobbying and Fraud Detection." *Journal of Financial and Quantitative Analysis* 46(06): 1865–91.

CHAPTER 4 CITATIONS

Alexander, Raquel Meyer, Stephen W. Mazza, and Susan Scholz. 2009. *Measuring Rates of Return for Lobbying Expenditures: An Empirical Case Study of Tax Breaks for Multinational Corporations*. Rochester, NY: Social Science Research Network. SSRN Scholarly Paper. https://papers.ssrn.com/abstract=1375082 (January 22, 2020).

Andres, Gary. 2009. *Lobbying Reconsidered: Politics under the Influence*. New York: Pearson Education.

Baumgartner, Frank R., Jeffrey M. Berry, Marie Hojnacki, David C. Kimball, and Beth L. Leech. 2009. *Lobbying and Policy Change: Who Wins, Who Loses, and Why*. Chicago: University of Chicago Press.

Baumgartner, Frank R., and Bryan D. Jones. 1993. *Agendas and Instability in American Politics,* 2nd ed. Chicago: University of Chicago Press.

Baumgartner, Frank R., Heather A. Larsen-Price, Beth L. Leech, and Paul Rutledge. 2011. "Congressional and Presidential Effects on the Demand for Lobbying." *Political Research Quarterly* 64(1): 3–16.

Baumgartner, Frank R., and Beth L. Leech. 1998. *Basic Interests: The Importance of Groups in Politics and in Political Science*. Princeton: Princeton University Press.

Boehmke, Frederick J., Sean Gailmard, and John W. Patty. 2013. "Business as Usual: Interest Group Access and Representation across Policy-Making Venues." *Journal of Public Policy* 33(1): 3–33.

Bullock, Charles S., and Karen L. Padgett. 2007. "Partisan Change and Consequences for Lobbying: Two-Party Government Comes to the Georgia Legislature." *State & Local Government Review* 39(2): 61–71.

Curry, James. 2015. *Legislating in the Dark*. Chicago: University of Chicago Press.

Drope, Jeffrey M., and Wendy L. Hansen. 2006. "Does Firm Size Matter? Analyzing Business Lobbying in the United States." *Business and Politics* 8(2): 1–17.

Drutman, Lee. 2015. *The Business of America Is Lobbying: How Corporations Became Politicized and Politics Became More Corporate*. Oxford: Oxford University Press.

Feinberg, Robbie. 2014. "Special Interests Heavily Involved in Farm Bill Maneuvering." *OpenSecrets,* January 30, 2014. https://www.opensecrets.org/news/2014/01/special-interests-heavily-involved/ (accessed June 22, 2021).

De Figueiredo, John M. 2002. "Lobbying and Information in Politics." *Business and Politics* 4(2): 125–29.

De Figueiredo, John M. 2004. *The Timing, Intensity, and Composition of Interest Group Lobbying: An Analysis of Structural Policy Windows in the States*. National Bureau of Economic Research. Working Paper. http://www.nber.org/papers/w10588 (accessed October 24, 2018).

De Figueiredo, John M., and Brian Kelleher Richter. 2013. *Advancing the Empirical Research on Lobbying*. National Bureau of Economic Research. Working Paper. http://www.nber.org/papers/w19698 (accessed March 28, 2014).

Fisher, Andrew. 2017. *Big Hunger: The Unholy Alliance between Corporate America and Anti-Hunger Groups*. Cambridge, MA: MIT Press.

Grossmann, Matt, and David A. Hopkins. 2016. *Asymmetric Politics: Ideological Republicans and Group Interest Democrats*. New York: Oxford University Press.

REFERENCES

Hall, Richard L., and Alan V. Deardorff. 2006. "Lobbying as Legislative Subsidy." *American Political Science Review* 100(1): 69–84.

Hansen, John Mark. 1991. *Gaining Access: Congress and the Farm Lobby, 1919–1981.* Chicago: University of Chicago Press.

Hojnacki, Marie, and David C. Kimball. 1998. "Organized Interests and the Decision of Whom to Lobby in Congress." *American Political Science Review* 92(4): 775–90.

Hojnacki, Marie, and David C. Kimball. 1999. "The Who and How of Organizations' Lobbying Strategies in Committee." *Journal of Politics* 61(04): 999–1024.

Holyoke, Thomas T. 2016. "Choosing Battlegrounds: Interest Group Lobbying across Multiple Venues." *Political Research Quarterly.* http://journals.sagepub.com/doi/10.1177/1065912903055600307 (accessed February 3, 2020).

Klein, Ezra, and Susannah Locke. 2014. "40 Maps That Explain Food in America." *Vox,* June 9, 2014. https://www.vox.com/a/explain-food-america (accessed January 29, 2020).

LaPira, Timothy M., and Herschel F. Thomas III. 2017. *Revolving Door Lobbying: Public Service, Private Influence, and the Unequal Representation of Interests.* Lawrence: University Press of Kansas.

LaPira, Timothy M., and Herschel F. Thomas III. 2020. "The Lobbying Disclosure Act at 25: Challenges and Opportunities for Analysis." *Interest Groups and Advocacy* 9: 257–71.

Leech, Beth L., Frank R. Baumgartner, Timothy M. La Pira, and Nicholas A. Semanko. 2005. "Drawing Lobbyists to Washington: Government Activity and the Demand for Advocacy." *Political Research Quarterly* 58(1): 19–30.

Lobbying Disclosure Act Guidance. 2013. Washington, DC: Senate Office of Public Records.

Lux, Sean, T. Russell Crook, and David J. Woehr. 2011. "Mixing Business with Politics: A Meta-Analysis of the Antecedents and Outcomes of Corporate Political Activity." *Journal of Management* 37(1): 223–47.

Mathur, Ike, and Manohar Singh. 2011. *Corporate Political Strategies.* Rochester, NY: Social Science Research Network. SSRN Scholarly Paper. http://papers.ssrn.com/abstract=1774328 (accessed November 4, 2013).

McConnell, Grant. 1966. *Private Power and American Democracy.* New York: Knopf.

McKay, Amy. 2012. "Buying Policy? The Effects of Lobbyists' Resources on Their Policy Success." *Political Research Quarterly* 65(4): 703–954.

McKay, Amy. 2018. "Fundraising for Favors? Linking Lobbyist-Hosted Fundraisers to Legislative Benefits." *Political Research Quarterly* 71(4): 869–80.

Ommundsen, Emily Cottle. 2022. "The Institution's Knowledge: Congressional Staff Experience and Committee Productivity." *Legislative Studies Quarterly* 48(2): 273–303. http://onlinelibrary.wiley.com/doi/abs/10.1111/lsq.12401 (accessed December 14, 2022).

Poole, Keith T., and Howard Rosenthal. 2006. *Ideology and Congress: A Political Economic History of Roll Call Voting.* 2nd ed. New Brunswick: Routledge.

Reiley, Laura. 2019. "Trump's $16 Billion Farm Bailout Will Make Rich Farmers Richer, Report Says." *Washington Post,* July 31, 2019. https://www.washingtonpost.com/business/2019/07/31/trumps-billion-farm-bailout-will-make-rich-farmers-richer-hasten-small-farm-failure-study-says/ (accessed February 7, 2020).

Rosenthal, Howard, and Keith Poole. 2015. "Political Polarization." *Voteview*. http://voteview.com/political_polarization_2014.html (accessed August 1, 2016).

Schattschneider, Elmer E. 1960. *The Semisovereign People: A Realist's View of Democracy in America*. rev. ed. Hinsdale, IL: Cengage Learning.

Theriault, Sean M. 2013. *The Gingrich Senators: The Roots of Partisan Warfare in Congress*. Oxford: Oxford University Press.

Waterhouse, Benjamin C. 2015. *Lobbying America: The Politics of Business from Nixon to NAFTA*. reprint ed. Princeton: Princeton University Press.

CHAPTER 5 CITATIONS

Abbott, Charles. 2008. "Congress Overrides Bush Veto of Farm Law—Again." *Reuters*, June 18, 2008. https://www.reuters.com/article/us-usa-agriculture-farmbill-idUSN18279220080618 (accessed December 2, 2022).

Abbott, Charles. 2013. "House Deals Shock Defeat to Republican Farm Bill." *Reuters*, June 20, 2013. https://www.reuters.com/article/us-usa-agriculture-idUKBRE95J10C20130620 (November 29, 2022).

Alexander, Raquel Meyer, Stephen W. Mazza, and Susan Scholz. 2009. *Measuring Rates of Return for Lobbying Expenditures: An Empirical Case Study of Tax Breaks for Multinational Corporations*. Rochester, NY: Social Science Research Network. SSRN Scholarly Paper. https://papers.ssrn.com/abstract=1375082 (accessed January 22, 2020).

Associated Press. 2015. "FDA Head Says Menu Labeling 'Thorny' Issue." *Fox News*, March 12, 2013. https://www.foxnews.com/health/fda-head-says-menu-labeling-thorny-issue (accessed December 7, 2022).

Baumgartner, Frank R., Jeffrey M. Berry, Marie Hojnacki, David C. Kimball, and Beth L. Leech. 2009. *Lobbying and Policy Change: Who Wins, Who Loses, and Why*. Chicago: University of Chicago Press.

Baumgartner, Frank R., and Beth L. Leech. 2001. "Interest Niches and Policy Bandwagons: Patterns of Interest Group Involvement in National Politics." *Journal of Politics* 63(04): 1191–1213.

"Bills: 2013." n.d. Lobbying Spending Database, Center for Responsive Politics. https://www.opensecrets.org/lobby/top.php?indexType=b&showYear=2013 (accessed March 21, 2017).

Binder, Sarah A. 1999. "The Dynamics of Legislative Gridlock, 1947-96." *American Political Science Review* 93(3): 519–33.

Black, Earl, and Merle Black. 2007. *Divided America: The Ferocious Power Struggle in American Politics*. reprint ed. Simon & Schuster.

Boehmke, Frederick J. 2005. *Indirect Effect of Direct Legislation: How Institutions Shape Interest Group Systems*. Columbus: Ohio State University Press.

Bosso, Christopher J. 2017. *Framing the Farm Bill: Interests, Ideology, and Agricultural Act of 2014*. Lawrence: University Press of Kansas.

Brewer, Mark D. 2005. "The Rise of Partisanship and the Expansion of Partisan Conflict within the American Electorate." *Political Research Quarterly* 58(2): 219–29.

Brock, Clare. 2021. "Partisan Polarization and Corporate Lobbying: Information, Demand, and Conflict." *Interest Groups & Advocacy*. https://doi.org/10.1057/s41309-021-00112-5 (accessed March 25, 2021).

REFERENCES

Browne, William P. 1990. "Organized Interests and Their Issue Niches: A Search for Pluralism in a Policy Domain." *Journal of Politics* 52(2): 477–509.

Bush, George W. 2008. "Farm Bill Veto Message." *The White House,* May 21, 2008. https://georgewbush-whitehouse.archives.gov/news/releases/2008/05/20080521-4.html (accessed December 5, 2022).

"Comparative Agendas Project: United States." *Comparative Agendas Project.* http://www.comparativeagendas.net/ (accessed September 6, 2016).

Drutman, Lee. 2015. *The Business of America Is Lobbying: How Corporations Became Politicized and Politics Became More Corporate.* Oxford: Oxford University Press.

Dusso, Aaron. 2010. "Legislation, Political Context, and Interest Group Behavior." *Political Research Quarterly* 63(1): 55–67.

Eisenhower, Dwight D. 1956. "Veto of the Farm Bill." *The American Presidency Project.* https://www.presidency.ucsb.edu/documents/veto-the-farm-bill (accessed December 5, 2022).

Fagan, Edward James. 2020. "Information Wars: Party Elites, Think Tanks and Polarization in Congress." Thesis. https://repositories.lib.utexas.edu/handle/2152/85635 (accessed June 24, 2021).

de Figueiredo, John M. 2002. "Lobbying and Information in Politics." *Business and Politics* 4(2): 125–29.

de Figueiredo, John M. 2004. *The Timing, Intensity, and Composition of Interest Group Lobbying: An Analysis of Structural Policy Windows in the States.* National Bureau of Economic Research. Working Paper. http://www.nber.org/papers/w10588 (accessed October 24, 2018).

Food, Conservation, and Energy Act of 2008 (Public Law No. 110–234, H.R. 2419, 122 Stat. 923), Actions. 2008. https://www.congress.gov/bill/110th-congress/house-bill/2419/all-actions (accessed December 5, 2022).

Garlick, Alex. 2021. "Interest Group Lobbying and Partisan Polarization in the United States: 1999–2016." *Political Science Research and Methods*: 1–19.

Good, Keith. 2014. "President Obama Signs 2014 Farm Bill into Law." *Farm Policy.* http://farmpolicy.com/2014/02/08/weekend-update-president-obama-signs-2014-farm-bill-into-law/ (accessed March 2, 2017).

Gray, Virginia, John Culveris, Jeffrey J. Harden, Boris Shor, and David Lowery. 2015. "Party Competition, Party Polarization, and the Changing Demand for Lobbying in the American States." *American Politics Research* 43(2): 175–204.

Herszenhorn, David M., and David Stout. 2008. "Defying President Bush, Senate Passes Farm Bill." *New York Times,* May 15, 2008. https://www.nytimes.com/2008/05/15/washington/15cnd-farm.html (accessed December 5, 2022).

Huber, John D., Charles R. Shipan, and Madelaine Pfahler. 2001. "Legislatures and Statutory Control of Bureaucracy." *American Journal of Political Science* 45(2): 330–45.

LaPira, Timothy M., and Herschel F. Thomas III. 2017. *Revolving Door Lobbying: Public Service, Private Influence, and the Unequal Representation of Interests.* Lawrence: University Press of Kansas.

Layman, Geoffrey C., Thomas M. Carsey, John C. Green, Richard Herrera, and Rosalyn Cooperman. 2010. "Activists and Conflict Extension in American Party Politics." *American Political Science Review* 104(2): 324–46.

Lowery, David, Virginia Gray, Justin Kirkland, and Jeffrey J. Harden. 2012. "Generalist Interest Organizations and Interest System Density: A Test of the Competitive Exclusion Hypothesis." *Social Science Quarterly* 1(93): 21–41.

Neely, Brett. 2013. "Farm Bill Heads to Full Senate, Prospects in House Dim." *Minnesota Public Radio News,* June 6, 2013. http://www.mprnews.org/story/2013/06/06/politics/farm-bill-senate (accessed March 21, 2017).

Plotnick, Robert D., and Richard F. Winters. 1990. "Party, Political Liberalism, and Redistribution: An Application to the American States." *American Politics Quarterly* 18(4): 430–58.

Poole, Keith T., and Howard Rosenthal. 2000. *Congress: A Political-Economic History of Roll Call Voting.* New York: Oxford University Press.

Rosenthal, Howard, and Keith Poole. 2015. "Political Polarization." *Voteview.* http://voteview.com/political_polarization_2014.html (accessed August 1, 2016).

Schattschneider, Elmer E. 1960. *The Semisovereign People: A Realist's View of Democracy in America.* rev. ed. Hinsdale, IL: Cengage Learning.

Sheingate, Adam. 2013. "The Future of Farm Bills." *The Monkey Cage,* June 28, 2013. http://themonkeycage.org/2013/06/the-future-of-farm-bills/ (accessed March 8, 2017).

Sinclair, Barbara. 2006. *Party Wars: Polarization and the Politics of National Policy Making.* Norman: University of Oklahoma Press.

Theriault, Sean M. 2013. *The Gingrich Senators: The Roots of Partisan Warfare in Congress.* Oxford: Oxford University Press.

Waterhouse, Benjamin C. 2015. *Lobbying America: The Politics of Business from Nixon to NAFTA.* Reprint ed. Princeton: Princeton University Press.

Wilson, Duff, and Janet Roberts. 2012. "Special Report: How Washington Went Soft on Childhood Obesity." *Reuters,* April 27, 2012. https://www.reuters.com/article/us-usa-foodlobby-idUSBRE83Q0ED20120427 (accessed December 1, 2022).

"With Defeat of 2013 Farm Bill, House Fails Soybean Farmers and American Agriculture." 2013. American Soybean Association, June 20, 2013. https://soygrowers.com/news-releases/with-defeat-of-2013-farm-bill-house-fails-soybean-farmers-and-american-agriculture/ (accessed November 30, 2022).

CHAPTER 6 CITATIONS

Alexander, Raquel Meyer, Stephen W. Mazza, and Susan Scholz. 2009. *Measuring Rates of Return for Lobbying Expenditures: An Empirical Case Study of Tax Breaks for Multinational Corporations.* Rochester, NY: Social Science Research Network. SSRN Scholarly Paper. https://papers.ssrn.com/abstract=1375082 (accessed January 22, 2020).

Andres, Gary. 2009. *Lobbying Reconsidered: Politics under the Influence.* New York: Routledge.

Austen-Smith, David, and Jeffrey S. Banks. 2000. "Cheap Talk and Burned Money." *Journal of Economic Theory* 91(1): 1–16.

Baumgartner, Frank R., Jeffrey M. Berry, Marie Hojnacki, David C. Kimball, and Beth L. Leech 2009. *Lobbying and Policy Change: Who Wins, Who Loses, and Why.* Chicago: University of Chicago Press.

REFERENCES

Baumgartner, Frank R., and Beth L. Leech. 1998. *Basic Interests: The Importance of Groups in Politics and in Political Science.* Princeton: Princeton University Press.

Bertrand, Marianne, Matilde Bombardini, and Francesco Trebbi. 2014. "Is It Whom You Know or What You Know? An Empirical Assessment of the Lobbying Process." *American Economic Review* 104(12): 3885–3920.

Browne, William P. 1988. *Private Interests, Public Policy, and American Agriculture.* Lawrence: University Press of Kansas.

Browne, William P. 1995. *Cultivating Congress: Constituents, Issues, and Interests in Agricultural Policymaking.* Lawrence University Press of Kansas.

Curry, James. 2015. *Legislating in the Dark.* Chicago: University of Chicago Press.

DeGregorio, Christine A. 2010. *Networks of Champions: Leadership, Access, and Advocacy in the U.S. House of Representatives.* Ann Arbor: University of Michigan Press.

Drutman, Lee. 2015. *The Business of America Is Lobbying: How Corporations Became Politicized and Politics Became More Corporate.* Oxford: Oxford University Press.

Dusso, Aaron. 2010. "Legislation, Political Context, and Interest Group Behavior." *Political Research Quarterly* 63(1): 55–67.

Dwidar, Maraam. 2022. "Diverse Lobbying Coalitions and Influence in Notice-and-Comment Rulemaking." *Policy Studies Journal* 50(1): 199–240.

Esteban, Joan, and Debraj Ray. 2006. "Inequality, Lobbying, and Resource Allocation." *American Economic Review* 96(1): 257–79.

Fagan, E. J., Zachary A. McGee, and Herschel F. Thomas. 2021. "The Power of the Party: Conflict Expansion and the Agenda Diversity of Interest Groups." *Political Research Quarterly* 74(1): 90–102.

Franklin, George. 2014. *Raisin Bran and Other Cereal Wars: 30 Years of Lobbying for the Most Famous Tiger in the World.* Bloomington, IN: iUniverse.

Good, Keith. 2014. "President Obama Signs 2014 Farm Bill into Law." *Farm Policy.* http://farmpolicy.com/2014/02/08/weekend-update-president-obama-signs-2014-farm-bill-into-law/ (accessed March 2, 2017).

Hall, Richard L., and Alan V. Deardorff. 2006. "Lobbying as Legislative Subsidy." *American Political Science Review* 100(1): 69–84.

Hall, Richard L., and Frank W. Wayman. 1990. "Buying Time: Moneyed Interests and the Mobilization of Bias in Congressional Committees." *American Political Science Review* 84(3): 797–820.

Hansen, John Mark. 1991. *Gaining Access: Congress and the Farm Lobby, 1919–1981.* Chicago: University of Chicago Press.

Klein, Ezra. 2013. "The Most Depressing Graphic for Members of Congress." *Washington Post,* January 14, 2013. https://www.washingtonpost.com/news/wonk/wp/2013/01/14/the-most-depressing-graphic-for-members-of-congress/ (accessed March 24, 2021).

Koerth, Maggie. 2019. "Everyone Knows Money Influences Politics . . . Except Scientists." *FiveThirtyEight,* June 4, 2019. https://fivethirtyeight.com/features/everyone-knows-money-influences-politics-except-scientists/ (accessed April 14, 2021).

LaPira, Timothy M., and Herschel F. Thomas III. 2017. *Revolving Door Lobbying: Public Service, Private Influence, and the Unequal Representation of Interests.* Lawrence: University Press of Kansas.

Lee, Frances E. 2016. *Insecure Majorities: Congress and the Perpetual Campaign*. Chicago: University of Chicago Press.

McCarty, Nolan M., Keith T. Poole, and Howard Rosenthal. 2008. *Polarized America: The Dance of Ideology and Unequal Riches*. Cambridge, : MIT Press.

McKay, Amy. 2012. "Negative Lobbying and Policy Outcomes." *American Politics Research* 40(1): 116–46.

McKay, Amy. 2018. "Fundraising for Favors? Linking Lobbyist-Hosted Fundraisers to Legislative Benefits." *Political Research Quarterly* 71(4): 869–80.

McKay, Amy Melissa. 2020. "Buying Amendments? Lobbyists' Campaign Contributions and Microlegislation in the Creation of the Affordable Care Act." *Legislative Studies Quarterly* 45(2): 327–60.

Parker, Ashley. 2014. "Lawmakers Are Roommates No More." *New York Times*, December 16, 2014. https://www.nytimes.com/2014/12/17/us/after-decades-lawmak ers-are-roommates-no-more.html (accessed December 7, 2022).

Plotnick, Robert D., and Richard F. Winters. 1990. "Party, Political Liberalism, and Redistribution: An Application to the American States." *American Politics Quarterly* 18(4): 430–58.

Reynolds, Molly. 2021. *Vital Statistics on Congress*. Brookings Institution. https://www. brookings.edu/wp-content/uploads/2019/03/Chpt-5.pdf.

Sheingate, Adam. 2013. "The Future of Farm Bills." *The Monkey Cage,* June 28, 2013. http://themonkeycage.org/2013/06/the-future-of-farm-bills/ (accessed March 8, 2017).

Sheingate, Adam D. 2003. *The Rise of the Agricultural Welfare State: Institutions and Interest Group Power in the United States, France, and Japan*. Princeton: Princeton University Press.

Tripathi, Micky, Stephen Ansolabehere, and James M. Snyder. 2017. "Are PAC Contributions and Lobbying Linked? New Evidence from the 1995 Lobby Disclosure Act." *Business and Politics* 4(2): 131–55.

Chapter 7 Citations

Baumgartner, Frank, and Bryan Jones. 2015. *The Politics of Information*. Chicago: University of Chicago Press.

Baumgartner, Frank R., Jeffrey M. Berry, Marie Hojnacki, David C. Kimball, and Beth L. Leech. 2009. *Lobbying and Policy Change: Who Wins, Who Loses, and Why*. Chicago: University of Chicago Press.

Baumgartner, Frank R., and Bryan D. Jones. 1993. *Agendas and Instability in American Politics*. 2nd ed. Chicago: University of Chicago Press.

Bertrand, Marianne, Matilde Bombardini, and Francesco Trebbi. 2014. "Is It Whom You Know or What You Know? An Empirical Assessment of the Lobbying Process." *American Economic Review* 104(12): 3885–3920.

Binder, Sarah A. 1999. "The Dynamics of Legislative Gridlock, 1947-96." *American Political Science Review* 93(3): 519–33.

Butler, Daniel M., and David R. Miller. 2021. "Does Lobbying Affect Bill Advancement? Evidence from Three State Legislatures." *Political Research Quarterly* 75(3): 547–61.

Committee on the Budget. 2018. *Focus on Function 350—Agriculture*. Washington, DC: House Committee on the Budget. https://budget.house.gov/focus-function-350-agriculture-0 (accessed May 27, 2021).

Curry, James. 2015. *Legislating in the Dark*. Chicago: University of Chicago Press.

Davis, Kathleen, and Clare Brock. 2020. "Nutrition Practices to Grow Healthy Communities." In *Sustainable Community Health: Systems and Practices in Diverse Settings*, ed. Elias Mpofu. Cham: Springer International Publishing, 145–99. https://doi.org/10.1007/978-3-030-59687-3_5 (accessed July 8, 2021).

Dewey, Caitlin, and Erica Werner. 2018. "Senate Overwhelmingly Passes Sweeping Farm Bill, Setting up Fight with House." *Washington Post,* June 28, 2018. https://www.washingtonpost.com/business/economy/senate-passes-sweeping-farm-bill-setting-up-fight-with-house/2018/06/28/0007d532-7aff-11e8-80be-6d32e182a3bc_story.html (accessed March 1, 2023).

Drope, Jeffrey M., and Wendy L. Hansen. 2006. "Does Firm Size Matter? Analyzing Business Lobbying in the United States." *Business and Politics* 8(2): 1–17.

Drutman, Lee. 2015. *The Business of America Is Lobbying: How Corporations Became Politicized and Politics Became More Corporate*. Oxford: Oxford University Press.

Esterling, Kevin M. 2004. *The Political Economy of Expertise: Information and Efficiency in American National Politics*. Ann Arbor: University of Michigan Press.

Hall, Richard L., and Alan V. Deardorff. 2006. "Lobbying as Legislative Subsidy." *American Political Science Review* 100(1): 69–84.

Hojnacki, Marie, and David C. Kimball. 1998. "Organized Interests and the Decision of Whom to Lobby in Congress." *American Political Science Review* 92(4): 775–90.

Hughes, Tyler, and Deven Carlson. 2015. "Divided Government and Delay in the Legislative Process: Evidence from Important Bills, 1949–2010." *American Politics Research* 43(5): 771–92.

LaPira, Timothy M., and Herschel F. Thomas III. 2017. *Revolving Door Lobbying: Public Service, Private Influence, and the Unequal Representation of Interests*. Lawrence: University Press of Kansas.

Layman, Geoffrey C., Thomas M. Carsey, John C. Green, Richard Herrera, and Rosalyn Cooperman. 2010. "Activists and Conflict Extension in American Party Politics." *American Political Science Review* 104(2): 324–46.

Lewallen, Jonathan. 2020. *Committees and the Decline of Lawmaking in Congress*. Ann Arbor: University of Michigan Press.

Lindblom, Charles E. 1980. *Politics and Markets: The World's Political-Economic Systems*. New ed. New York: Basic Books.

McKay, Amy. 2012. "Buying Policy? The Effects of Lobbyists' Resources on Their Policy Success." *Political Research Quarterly* 65(4): 908–23.

"New USDA Rules Would Remove Junk Food from School Vending Machines." *CBSNews,* February 1, 2013. https://www.cbsnews.com/news/new-usda-rules-would-remove-junk-food-from-school-vending-machines/ (accessed May 27, 2021).

Nixon, Ron. 2012. "New Guidelines Planned on School Vending Machines." *New York Times,* February 20, 2013. https://www.nytimes.com/2012/02/21/us/politics/new-rules-planned-on-school-vending-machines.html (accessed May 27, 2021).

Schattschneider, Elmer E. 1960. *The Semisovereign People: A Realist's View of Democracy in America.* rev. ed. Hinsdale, IL: Cengage Learning.

Sternberg, Rugh. n.d. "Mending Vending." *AASA | American Association of School Administrators.* https://aasa.org/SchoolAdministratorArticle.aspx?id=7778 (accessed May 27, 2021).

CHAPTER 8 CITATIONS

Alexander, Raquel Meyer, Stephen W. Mazza, and Susan Scholz. 2009. "Measuring Rates of Return for Lobbying Expenditures: An Empirical Case Study of Tax Breaks for Multinational Corporations." Rochester, NY: Social Science Research Network. SSRN Scholarly Paper. https://papers.ssrn.com/abstract=1375082 (accessed January 22, 2020).

Bauer, Raymond Augustine, Ithiel de Sola Pool, and Lewis Anthony Dexter. 1963. *American Business and Public Policy: The Politics of Foreign Trade.* Atherton: Atherton Press.

Baumgartner, Frank R., Jeffrey M. Berry, Marie Hojnacki, Beth L. Leech, and David C. Kimball. 2009. *Lobbying and Policy Change: Who Wins, Who Loses, and Why.* Chicago: University of Chicago Press.

Baumgartner, Frank R., and Bryan D. Jones. 1993. *Agendas and Instability in American Politics.* Chicago: University of Chicago Press.

Beckel, Michael. 2017. *The Price of Power: A Deep-Dive Analysis into How Political Parties Squeeze Influential Lawmakers to Boost Campaign Coffers.* Washington, DC: Issue One. https://www.issueone.org/wp-content/uploads/2017/05/price-of-power-final.pdf.

Binder, Sarah A. 1999. "The Dynamics of Legislative Gridlock, 1947-96." *American Political Science Review* 93(3): 519–33.

Boehmke, Frederick J., Sean Gailmard, and John W. Patty. 2013. "Business as Usual: Interest Group Access and Representation across Policy-Making Venues." *Journal of Public Policy* 33(1): 3–33.

Bosso, Christopher J. 2017. *Framing the Farm Bill: Interests, Ideology, and Agricultural Act of 2014.* Lawrence: University Press of Kansas.

Brasher, Philip, Ben Nuelle, and Noah Wicks. 2021. "Coronavirus Food Assistance Program: Where Did the Money Go?" *AgriPulse*, March 3, 2021. https://www.agri-pulse.com/articles/15429-coronavirus-food-assistance-program-where-did-the-money-go?v=preview (accessed July 26, 2021).

Brock, Clare R., and Daniel Mallinson. Forthcoming. "Measuring the Stasis: Punctuated Equilibrium Theory and Partisan Polarization" *Policy Studies Journal.*

Caygle, Heather. @heatherscope. August 12, 2021. "Big Hill Campus News Here: For the First Time Ever, Staff Can Now Make More than Members of Congress." Twitter. https://twitter.com/heatherscope/status/1425876538285821955 (accessed August 27, 2021).

Charles, Dan. 2016. "Congress Just Passed a GMO Labeling Bill. Nobody's Super Happy About It." *NPR*, August 14, 2016. https://www.npr.org/sections/thesalt/2016/07/14/486060866/congress-just-passed-a-gmo-labeling-bill-nobodys-super-happy-about-it (accessed July 27, 2021).

REFERENCES

"Coronavirus Food Assistance Program 2 Data." 2020. Farmers.gov. https://www.farmers.gov/cfap2/data (accessed July 26, 2021).

Curry, James. 2015. *Legislating in the Dark*. Chicago: University of Chicago Press.

Davis, Susan, Claudia Grisales, and Kelsey Snell. 2020. "Senate Passes $2 Trillion Coronavirus Relief Package." *NPR,* March 25, 2020. https://www.npr.org/2020/03/25/818881845/senate-reaches-historic-deal-on-2t-coronavirus-economic-rescue-package (accessed October 27, 2022).

Desilver, Drew. 2019. "A Productivity Scorecard for the 115th Congress: More Laws than before, but Not More Substance." *Pew Research Center,* January 5, 2019. https://www.pewresearch.org/fact-tank/2019/01/25/a-productivity-scorecard-for-115th-congress/ (accessed July 27, 2021).

Dwidar, Maraam A. 2021. "Diverse Lobbying Coalitions and Influence in Notice-and-Comment Rulemaking." *Policy Studies Journal* 50(1): 199–240. https://onlinelibrary.wiley.com/doi/abs/10.1111/psj.12431 (accessed July 28, 2021).

Fagan, E. J. 2020. "Information Wars: Party Elites, Think Tanks and Polarization in Congress." Thesis. https://repositories.lib.utexas.edu/handle/2152/85635 (accessed June 24, 2021).

Fagan, E. J., Zachary A. McGee, and Herschel F. Thomas. 2021. "The Power of the Party: Conflict Expansion and the Agenda Diversity of Interest Groups." *Political Research Quarterly* 74(1): 90–102.

Garlick, Alex. 2021. "Interest Group Lobbying and Partisan Polarization in the United States: 1999–2016." *Political Science Research and Methods*: 1–19.

"GMO Crops, Animal Food, and Beyond." 2020. *FDA.* https://www.fda.gov/food/agricultural-biotechnology/gmo-crops-animal-food-and-beyond (accessed July 28, 2021).

Golshan, Tara. 2018. "A House Revolt over Immigration Just Killed the Farm Bill—for Now." *Vox,* May 18, 2018. https://www.vox.com/2018/5/18/17368178/farm-bill-2018-fails-immigration-daca-house (accessed July 27, 2021).

Gray, Virginia, John Cluverius, Jeffrey J. Harden, Boris Shor, and David Lowery. 2015. "Party Competition, Party Polarization, and the Changing Demand for Lobbying in the American States." *American Politics Research* 43(2): 175–204.

Hall, Richard L., and Alan V. Deardorff. 2006. "Lobbying as Legislative Subsidy." *American Political Science Review* 100(1): 69–84.

Hansen, John Mark. 1991. *Gaining Access: Congress and the Farm Lobby, 1919–1981.* Chicago: University of Chicago Press.

Harris, Rebecca. 2016. "The Political Identity of Food: Partisan Implications of the New Food Politics." *Food Studies: An Interdisciplinary Journal* 6(4): 1–20.

Hojnacki, Marie. 1997. "Interest Groups' Decisions to Join Alliances or Work Alone." *American Journal of Political Science* 41(1): 61–87.

Jalonick, Mary Clare. 2015. "Poll Finds Most Americans Want GMO Food Labels." PBS News Hour. https://www.pbs.org/newshour/nation/poll-finds-americans-support-gmo-food-labeling (accessed July 28, 2021).

Klein, Ezra. 2013. "The Most Depressing Graphic for Members of Congress." *Washington Post,* January 13, 2015. https://www.washingtonpost.com/news/wonk/wp/2013/01/14/the-most-depressing-graphic-for-members-of-congress/ (accessed March 24, 2021).

Kurtz, Glen. 2001. *Hitching a Ride: Omnibus Legislating in the U.S. Congress*. Columbus: Ohio State University Press.

LaPira, Timothy M., and Herschel F. Thomas III. 2017. *Revolving Door Lobbying: Public Service, Private Influence, and the Unequal Representation of Interests*. Lawrence: University Press of Kansas.

Lipton, Eric. 2015. "Food Industry Enlisted Academics in G.M.O. Lobbying War, Emails Show." *New York Times,* September 5, 2015. https://www.nytimes.com/2015/09/06/us/food-industry-enlisted-academics-in-gmo-lobbying-war-emails-show.html (accessed July 27, 2021).

Mason, Lilliana. 2018. *Uncivil Agreement: How Politics Became Our Identity*. Chicago: University of Chicago Press.

Nelson, David, and Susan Webb Yackee. 2012. "Lobbying Coalitions and Government Policy Change: An Analysis of Federal Agency Rulemaking." *Journal of Politics* 74(2): 339–53.

Newton, John. 2018. "Who Supported the Farm Bill?" *Farm Bureau Market Intel,* December 19, 2018. https://www.fb.org/market-intel/who-supported-the-farm-bill (accessed July 27, 2021).

"Public Opinion about Genetically Modified Foods and Trust in Scientists Connected to These Foods." 2016. *Pew Research Center Science & Society,* December 1, 2016. https://www.pewresearch.org/science/2016/12/01/public-opinion-about-genetically-modified-foods-and-trust-in-scientists-connected-with-these-foods/ (accessed July 28, 2021).

Ramgopal, Kit. 2019. "Trump's Trade War Squeezes the Juice out of Maine's Wild Blueberry Business." *NBC News,* November 28, 2019. https://www.nbcnews.com/news/all/trumps-trade-war-squeezes-juice-out-maine-s-wild-n1091941 (accessed July 26, 2021).

Ramgopal, Kit. 2020. "New Coronavirus Bailout for Farms Will Have Winners and Losers." *NBC News,* May 19, 2020. https://www.nbcnews.com/business/economy/government-has-earmarked-billions-help-farmers-there-will-be-winners-n1209346 (accessed July 26, 2021).

Ramgopal, Kit, and Andrew W. Lehren. 2020. "Small Farmers Left behind in COVID-19 Relief Package." *NBC News,* August 9, 2020. https://www.nbcnews.com/business/economy/small-farmers-left-behind-trump-administration-s-covid-19-relief-n1236158 (accessed July 26, 2021).

Reiley, Laura. 2021. "Relief Bill Is Most Significant Legislation for Black Farmers since Civil Rights Act, Experts Say." *Washington Post,* March 8, 2021. https://www.washingtonpost.com/business/2021/03/08/reparations-black-farmers-stimulus/ (accessed October 27, 2022).

Snell, Kelsey, and Brian Naylor. 2018. "House Farm Bill Fails as Conservatives Revolt over Immigration." *NPR,* May 18, 2018. https://www.npr.org/2018/05/18/612203191/house-farm-bill-in-jeopardy-as-leaders-court-conservatives.

Sprunt, Barbara. 2021. "Here's What's in the American Rescue Plan." *NPR,* March 11, 2021. https://www.npr.org/sections/coronavirus-live-updates/2021/03/09/974841565/heres-whats-in-the-american-rescue-plan-as-it-heads-toward-final-passage (accessed October 27, 2022).

REFERENCES

"States Are Using Much-Needed Temporary Flexibility in SNAP to Respond to COVID-19 Challenges." 2022. *Center on Budget and Policy Priorities.* https://www.cbpp.org/research/food-assistance/states-are-using-much-needed-temporary-flexibility-in-snap-to-respond-to (accessed October 27, 2022).

"USDA Announces Coronavirus Food Assistance Program." *USDA,* April 17, 2020. https://www.usda.gov/media/press-releases/2020/04/17/usda-announces-coronavirus-food-assistance-program (accessed July 26, 2021).

Vital Statistics on Congress. 2021. Brookings Institution. https://www.brookings.edu/multi-chapter-report/vital-statistics-on-congress/ (accessed March 31, 2021).

Wise, Lindsay. 2015. "GMO Labeling Is at the Center of a Congressional Food Fight." *Washington Post,* July 12, 2015. https://www.washingtonpost.com/politics/gmo-labeling-is-at-the-center-of-a-congressional-food-fight/2015/07/12/881d8058-24cb-11e5-b72c-2b7d516e1e0e_story.html (July 27, 2021).

APPENDIX A

Drutman, Lee. 2015. *The Business of America Is Lobbying: How Corporations Became Politicized and Politics Became More Corporate.* Oxford: Oxford University Press.

de Figueiredo, John M., and Brian Kelleher Richter. 2014. "Advancing the Empirical Research on Lobbying." *Annual Review of Political Science* 17(1): 163–85.

Hojnacki, Marie, and David C. Kimball. 1998. "Organized Interests and the Decision of Whom to Lobby in Congress." *American Political Science Review* 92(4): 775–90.

Hojnacki, Marie, and David C. Kimball. 1999. "The Who and How of Organizations' Lobbying Strategies in Committee." *Journal of Politics* 61(4): 999–1024.

LaPira, Timothy M., and Herschel F. Thomas III. 2020. "The Lobbying Disclosure Act at 25: Challenges and Opportunities for Analysis." *Interest Groups & Advocacy* 9(3): 257–71.

LaPira, Timothy M., and Herschel F. Thomas III. 2017. *Revolving Door Lobbying: Public Service, Private Influence, and the Unequal Representation of Interests.* Lawrence: University Press of Kansas.

Lux, Sean, T. Russell Crook, and David J. Woehr. 2011. "Mixing Business with Politics: A Meta-Analysis of the Antecedents and Outcomes of Corporate Political Activity." *Journal of Management* 37(1): 223–47.

Mathur, Ike, and Manohar Singh. 2011. "Corporate Political Strategies." *Accounting & Finance* 51(1): 252–77.

Office of the Clerk, U.S. House of Representatives. 2021. "Lobbying Disclosure Act Guidance." https://lobbyingdisclosure.house.gov/amended_lda_guide.html (accessed December 15, 2022).

WRDS Compustat North America (via Wharton). https://library.maastrichtuniversity.nl/database/compuna/#:~:text=publicly%20held%20companies.-,Database%20info,Flows%2C%20and%20supplemental%20data%20items (accessed 2015).

INDEX

For the benefit of digital users, indexed terms that span two pages (e.g., 52–53) may, on occasion, appear on only one of those pages.

Tables and figures are indicated by *t* and *f* following the page number

Aderholt, Robert, 4–5

adjunct staffers (lobbyists as), 10–11, 31–32, 50–51, 55–60, 111

agenda setting, 36–37, 45–46

agenda crowding, 68–69, 147

agenda expansion, 83–84

Agendas and Instability, 42

agribusiness, 60–61, 70–71, 110–14

agriculture extension office, 21–22

air cover, 102–8, 125–26, 129–31, 138

American Beverage Association, 122

American Frozen Food Institute, 3–4

American Heart Association, 5

American Rescue Plan, 138

American Medical Association, 5

American Soybean Association, 80

anti-hunger activisits / lobby, 2, 8, 10, 39–40, 72, 82, 131, 134–36

appropriations process, 4–5, 138–39

bandwagon effect (Bandwagoning), 45–46, 68–69, 71, 105, 118*t*

Baumgartner, Frank, 95, 105

bipartisan, 2–3, 5–6, 11, 30, 38–39, 41–42, 43, 48–49, 51–52, 63, 78–79, 99–100, 104, 107, 113–14, 128, 132, 133–34, 135–36, 137, 138

Bittman, Mark, 6–7

Boebert, Lauren, 8–9

Boehner, John, 79–80

Bosso, Christopher, 8, 79, 136

bureaucracy, 33–34, 61–62, 64*f*, 65–68, 66*t*, 68*f*, 70, 86, 87*f*, 87, 88*t*, 89, 112*t*, 120, 125–26, 146–47

Butz, Earl, 23–24

campaign, 31–32, 49, 50–51, 53–54, 58, 59–60, 129

campaign contributions, 33–38, 96, 97

perpetual campaign, 99–100, 124, 127

Cantor, Eric, 41–42, 80

Center for Responsive Politics (CRP) 143–44

Center for Science in the Public Interest, 5

Centers for Disease Control and Prevention (CDC), 89–90

coalition

coalition-building, 13, 14, 15–16, 44, 45–46, 51–53, 75, 102–8

coalitional subsidy, 51–52, 129–31

cross-cutting, 38–39, 40, 42, 125–26, 129

interest-diverse, 44, 107

Coca-Cola (Coke), 72, 120–21, 148

collegial / collegiality, 15–16, 48–49, 60–61, 104, 124

Collins, Susan, 3–4

commodity (crop, program, title), 1–2, 6–7, 19–20, 22, 23, 24–25, 26, 39–40, 60–61, 80–81, 100, 110, 137

commodities

cattle (beef), 40, 137

corn, 23–24, 40, 77–78, 137

dairy, 25–26, 30, 40, 137

commodities (*cont.*)
    ethanol, 77–78, 125–26
    sugar, 8, 30, 106
    sugar beet, 106
    wheat, 23–24, 27
communication subsidy, 48–51, 53–54, 60–61
conflict
    expansion, 5–6, 58, 77, 82–83, 84*t*, 87, 92–93, 94, 109
    scope, 58
Congress
    congressional (legislative) staff, 11, 12–13, 14, 17, 31–32, 46, 49–53, 50*f*, 59–60, 75, 82, 94–95, 97–99, 100–2, 103, 105–6, 110, 124, 127–29, 138–39, 140–41, 146, 151–53
    congressional support agencies, 31–32, 50, 50*f*, 127
Conner, Chuck, 43, 55
consensus, 29, 40, 42, 80, 105
conservation, 19–20, 21, 72
    conservation interests, 25
    conservation programs, 6–7, 24–25, 56
    Conservation Reserve Program (CRP), 24–25
    Conservation Security Program (CSP), 24–25
    conservation title, 19–20, 24–25
constituency, 36–37, 56, 69, 99, 149
constituency services, 49, 58, 59–60
Conte, Silvio, 48–49
Contract with America, 25–26
Coronavirus, 20, 136
    Coronavirus Aid, Relief, and Economic Security (CARES) Act, 136–37
    Families First Coronavirus Response (FFCRA) Act, 136–37
corporate lobbying (firm lobbying), 5, 8, 14–15, 17–18, 35–36, 43, 53–54, 55–75, 82–83, 89, 90, 97–98, 99–100, 110–12, 114, 115–23, 118*t*, 125–26, 128–29, 131, 134–35, 136, 138, 140–41, 144–45, 149, 151–52
crop insurance, 19–21, 56, 110

decoupling effort, 42
DeLauro, Rosa, 91
Democrats, 4–5, 9–10, 25–26, 28, 31, 41–42, 43, 46–47, 78–79, 80, 89–90, 103, 113–14, 120, · 129, 132–33, 135
devolution, 42, 113–14
discretion (bureaucratic), 90–91, 92–93
Dole, Robert, 38–39, 42

Durbin, Richard, 99–100

electioneering, 99–100
Emerson, Jo Ann, 90
energy, 19–20, 27, 41, 77–78
environmental groups, 5, 6–7, 8
Environmental Quality Incentives Program (EQIP), 24–25
executive branch. *See also* bureaucracy; white house

farm bill
    Agricultural Act of 1949 25–26
    Agricultural Act of 2014 9–10, 15, 56, 63, 77
    Agriculture Improvement Act of 2018 63, 135
    Agriculture Reform, Food, and Jobs Act of 2013 77, 80
    Farm Security and Rural Investment Act of 2002 27
    Federal Agriculture Improvement and Reform Act (FAIR) of 1996 25–27
    Federal Agriculture Reform and Risk Management Act 2014 41
    Food, Conservation, and Energy Act of 2008 27, 41, 77–78
    Freedom to Farm Bill, 25–26
    1973 Agriculture and Consumer Protection Act, 23–24
    1933 Agricultural Adjustment Act, 20–21
    Nutrition Reform and Work Opportunity Act of 2013 80
    Secret Farm Bill, 2013 6–7
farm bloc, 82
farm subsidies, 8, 72, 77
Federal Crop Insurance Corporation, 20–21
federal debt limit, 6
firm location, 69, 149
Fisher, Andrew, 134–35
Food Allergy Labeling and Consumer Protection Act of 2004 27
Food and Drug Administration, 85, 90–91, 146
Food Policy Coalition, 90
Food Safety and Modernization Act, 20, 28
Food Stamp Act of 1964 24
forestry, 19–20
Freedom Caucus, 9–10, 135
fundraising / dialing for dollars, 31–32, 34–35, 50–51, 73–74, 96, 99

Gingrich, Newt, 25–26, 38–39, 50

INDEX

Gingrich senators, 35–36
GMO foods, 132–34
grass-roots lobbying (advocacy), 43–44, 71
Great Depression, 20–22, 39–40
Green New Deal, 8–9
Greene, Marjorie Taylor, 48–49
gridlock, 13, 14, 15, 16–17, 45–48, 51, 53–54,
    62–63, 70, 85–86, 87, 92–93, 94, 104,
    107–8, 109, 110–11, 124, 127, 128, 130–31,
    133–34, 139
Grocery Manufacturers Association (GMA),
    72, 132–33

Hamburg, Margaret, 90–91
Hansen, John Mark, 8, 32–33
Harkin, Tom, 91
Healthy, Hunger-Free Kids Act, 2–6, 7, 9–10,
    20, 27, 55–56, 89–90
Heritage Foundation, 9–10, 51–52
Hoefner, Ferd, 43–44, 113–14
horticulture, 19–20
Hot lunch club, 21–22
House Agriculture Committee, 25–26, 31, 34–
    35, 56, 98, 135, 136
House Appropriations Committee, 4–5
House Ways and Means, 34–35
Hoyer, Steny, 78–79
Huelskamp, Tim, 46–47

information
    provision, 128
    restriction, 31–32, 38–39, 59–60
    subsidy, 33–38, 57–58, 60–61, 100
institutional capacity, 14, 15–16, 49, 50, 59–60,
    98–99, 100
institutional friction, 51
inter-group competition, 45–46
interest group
    advocacy, 17, 56, 131
    reputation, 43–44
    strategy, 17, 42
intra-branch conflict, 85, 87, 92–93
iron triangle, 10, 28, 48–49. See also subsystem

Kellogg, 72, 148

leadership (Leaders)
    congressional, 6, 31–32, 59–60, 104
    house, 9–10, 79, 80
Leech, Beth, 105
legislative champions, 102–3

legislative work subsidies, 14
Let's Move Campaign, 2–3, 89–90, 120–21
lobbying. See also information provision;
    information subsidy
    as insurance, 13, 84–85
    negative lobbying, 96–97 (see also
        status quo)
Lobbying Disclosure Act (LDA), 14–15, 26–27, 63,
    64, 70–71, 74–75, 143–44, 146, 152
    lobbying disclosure forms, 74–75
    lobbying reports, 63, 64f, 65–68, 68f, 70, 71,
        87f, 113f, 143–44, 145
lobbyist
    adjunct staff, 10–11, 31–32, 50–51, 59–60,
        110–11, 127–28
    contract, 74–75, 97–98, 114–20, 117f, 118t,
        122–23, 130
    in-house, 16–17, 74–75, 114–20, 117f, 118t
    revolving door (revolvers), 44, 52–53, 85,
        95, 101–2, 114–20, 140–41
    subject-matter experts, 101–2
Lucas, Frank, 6–7, 9–10, 41–42

McGovern-Dole Program, 38–39
McGovern, George, 38–39, 42
McKay, Amy, 96
Miller, George, 99–100
Monsanto, 56–57, 132

National Council of Farmer Cooperatives,
    47–43, 55
National School Lunch Act of 1946 23
National School Lunch Program (NSLP), 1–2,
    4–5, 22–23
    Commodity disposal, 22
National Security, 23, 38–39
National Sustainable Agriculture
    Coalition, 43–44
Negotiation Subsidy, 15–16, 102–8, 124–25
Nestlé, 72
New York Times, 6–7, 78–79, 122
Nixon, Richard (Nixon
    Administration), 23–24
nutrition programs, 6–7, 19–20, 24,
    39–40, 41–42, 77–78, 136. See also
    national school lunch program
Nutrition title, 7, 19–20, 25–26

Obama, Barack (Obama Administration), 2–3,
    5, 28, 41–42, 63, 89–90
Obama, Michelle, 2–3, 5, 89–90, 122

Obesity, 2–3, 73, 89–90, 121–22
Ocasio-Cortez, Alexandria, 8–9, 48–49
Office of Management and Budget, 14–15
omnibus legislation (bill), 19, 25, 47, 79, 81–82, 90, 132–33, 138–39
O'Neill, Tip, 48–49
organic, 17, 77–78, 131

Pelosi, Nancy, 48–49, 140–41
Pepsi, 72
Perdue, Sonny, 137
policy image, 60
policy outcomes, 12–13, 15, 16–17, 34–36, 37, 53–54, 73–74, 75, 80–81, 85–86, 95–97, 109, 131
policy windows, 58, 85
political action committee (PAC), 34–36
Pompeo, Mike, 132
Public Health Security and Bioterrorism Preparedness and Response Act of 2002 27

quid pro quo, 33–34, 36–37

rank-and-file members, 31–33, 38, 49, 50–51, 59–61, 98–99, 104–5, 127–28
Reagan, Ronald, 48–49
Republicans (GOP), 4–5, 9–10, 25–26, 28, 31, 38–39, 40–42, 43, 46–47, 50, 52, 53, 56, 58–59, 60–61, 63, 73, 77–79, 80, 89–90, 98–99, 102–3, 113–14, 120, 129, 132–33, 135, 136, 138. *See also* Tea Party
resource allocation, 87, 89, 112
resources (members of Congress), 49, 50–51, 59–60. *See also* congressional capacity
resources (lobbying groups), 51–52, 53–54, 57, 61–62, 69, 70–71, 72, 73, 75, 85–86, 87, 89, 95–96, 97, 111–16, 130, 140, 148, 149
Roberts, Pat, 6–7, 25–26
roll call (floor) vote, 41, 73–74

Safe and Accurate Food Labeling Act, 132
Deny Consumers the Right to Know Act (DARK Act), 132
Schattschneider, E.E. 82, 122–23
School Nutrition Association (SNA), 2–3, 4
Schumer, Charles, 99–100

Senate Appropriations Committee, 5
Senate Committee on Agriculture, Nutrition, and Forestry, 6–7, 42, 98
Sheingate, Adam, 8
Southerland, Steve, 41–42
Stutzman, Marlin, 41–42
subsystem, 13, 14, 17–18, 28–30, 31, 38–39, 42, 45–46, 56–57, 60, 72, 76, 81–84, 92, 93, 94–95, 125
subsystem instability, 42
supercommittee, 6–7
Supplemental Nutrition Assistance Program (SNAP), 9–10, 27, 41–42, 56, 72, 73, 77–78, 113–14, 132–33, 135–36, 137, 138–39

Tea Party, 28, 80. *See also* Republican
Toomey, Patrick J. 138
trade associations (groups, unions), 9–10, 56–57, 60, 61–62, 68–69, 99–100, 148, 149, 151–52
trade title, 19–20
Trump, Donald (Trump Administration, Trump Campaign), 5–6, 35–36

unholy alliance, 104, 134–35, 139. *See also* coalitions
unions, 76, 97–98
Unlikely bedfellows, 125–26, 134–35. *See also* coalitions
US Department of Agriculture (USDA) / Agriculture Department, 1–2, 3–5, 9–10, 22, 23, 73, 82, 89–90, 120–22, 136–37, 138–39

Voteview, 45, 148

Walmart, 72, 148
War Food Administration (WFA), 22
Wetlands Reserve Program (WRP), 24–25
White House, 2–3, 4–5, 22, 61–62, 64f, 65–68, 66t, 68f, 70, 71, 78–79, 86, 87f, 87, 88t, 89, 90, 92–93, 112t, 113–14, 146–47. *See also* executive branch
White House National Nutrition Conference, 22
Wildlife Habitat Incentives Program (WHIP), 24–25
work requirements, 6–7, 9–10, 41–42, 113–14